PENGUIN BOOKS
THE BEST OF SUDHIR DAR

Sudhir Dar was born in 1932 at Allahabad. He took a Master's degree in geography and worked as a broadcaster with All India Radio and later with Air India doing sales promotion. He came to cartooning in 1960, creating a witty, wordless cartoon series for the *Statesman* (Delhi and Calcutta). In 1967 he joined the *Hindustan Times* where he spent over two decades drawing political cartoons and a daily pocket cartoon called 'This Is It!'. He worked with the *Pioneer* in Delhi for the next seven years, before moving to the *Delhi Times*, a daily supplement of the *Times of India*. Dar's cartoons have also appeared in the *New York Times*, the *Washington Post* and *Saturday Review*. Mad Magazine once called him a 'Tasty Indian nut'.

The recipient of numerous national and international awards, Dar's poster calendar for Air India won honours at the 1980 International CLIO awards in the USA. He also represented India at the first International Cartoonists' Conference in London in 1970. Many of his originals are now part of private collections including those of Queen Elizabeth II, Lord Richard Attenborough, Henry Kissinger and the late Yehudi Menuhin.

Sudhir Dar is married and has two daughters. He lives in Delhi.

The
Best of
Sudhir Dar

PENGUIN BOOKS

An imprint of Penguin Random House

PENGUIN BOOKS

USA | Canada | UK | Ireland | Australia
New Zealand | India | South Africa | China | Singapore

Penguin Books is part of the Penguin Random House group of companies
whose addresses can be found at global.penguinrandomhouse.com

Published by Penguin Random House India Pvt. Ltd
4th Floor, Capital Tower 1, MG Road,
Gurugram 122 002, Haryana, India

Penguin
Random House
India

First published by Penguin Books India 2000

10 9 8 7 6 5 4 3

ISBN 9780141002460

Printed at Repro India Limited

www.penguin.co.in

MIX
Paper from
responsible sources
FSC® C047271

This is a legitimate digitally printed version of the book and therefore might not
have certain extra finishing on the cover.

Preface

Forty years ago, I walked nervously up the steps of the old *Statesman* building in New Delhi, carrying a bunch of five wordless cartoons. The meeting with the editor was brief; it was obvious that he had no time to look at my work. Next morning, however, when I opened the *Statesman*, there they were, on page three—large as life!

Whatever I am today as a professional cartoonist I owe to that Englishman—Evan Charlton, the last British editor of the *Statesman*. He picked me up when I was a nobody and put me on centrestage. It was a terrifying test—I could either swim or sink. Luckily, I survived.

Cartoons had fascinated me all through my years of adolescence and youth. But as a livelihood, it was a dangerous profession to enter. As a freelancer you couldn't survive; payments were pitifully low. For instance, my first contribution to the *Illustrated Weekly of India* brought me the princely sum of seventy-five rupees—for three cartoons. The lesson there for all young, aspiring cartoonists was—look for a more secure job. So I tried my hand at other professions, but was never really able to find my feet. In the late fifties and early sixties, when some of us were taking our first steps into this profession, you could count the political cartoonists in the country on the fingers of one hand. Today, the situation has certainly improved— you can count them on two hands!

My reference here is largely confined to the English language press. Regional cartoonists, particularly in the

South, offer a regular diet of humour and satire, but because of the language barrier, little or nothing is known of them or their work outside their areas of operation. Unfortunately, we are more familiar with American cartoonists than our own.

In the sixties, I spent seven years with the *Statesman* doing a zany, wordless pocket cartoon called 'Out of My Mind'. Then it was time to enter another arena—politics. The *Statesman* in those days was British-owned and the editor wanted 'no political cartoons, just pure humour'. In 1967 when I joined the *Hindustan Times* as a political cartoonist I was given a clear message by the editor there. 'Forget the *Statesman*,' he said. 'Those cartoons will not do here. We have a different audience and your cartoons will sail over the heads of our readers. HT has had a long tradition of political cartooning—just stick to politics.'

I did. But there was another little space that offered great scope for having a daily dig at 'life, just everyday life'—the pocket cartoon on page one, and thus was born 'This is it!'. In those four decades with HT, I saw seven editors come and go. Every few years a new man would occupy the chair and one had to build a new relationship all over again. With some it was warm and meaningful, with others not so delightful. The relationship between an editor and a cartoonist has to be a special one—it helps greatly if you're on the same wavelength.

This selection of two hundred cartoons is a mixed bag. Some are from my HT years, others from the *Pioneer* where I spent the nineties, and a choice of more recent work—focusing on the jeans generation—from *Delhi Times*.

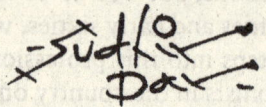

The
Best of
Sudhir Dar

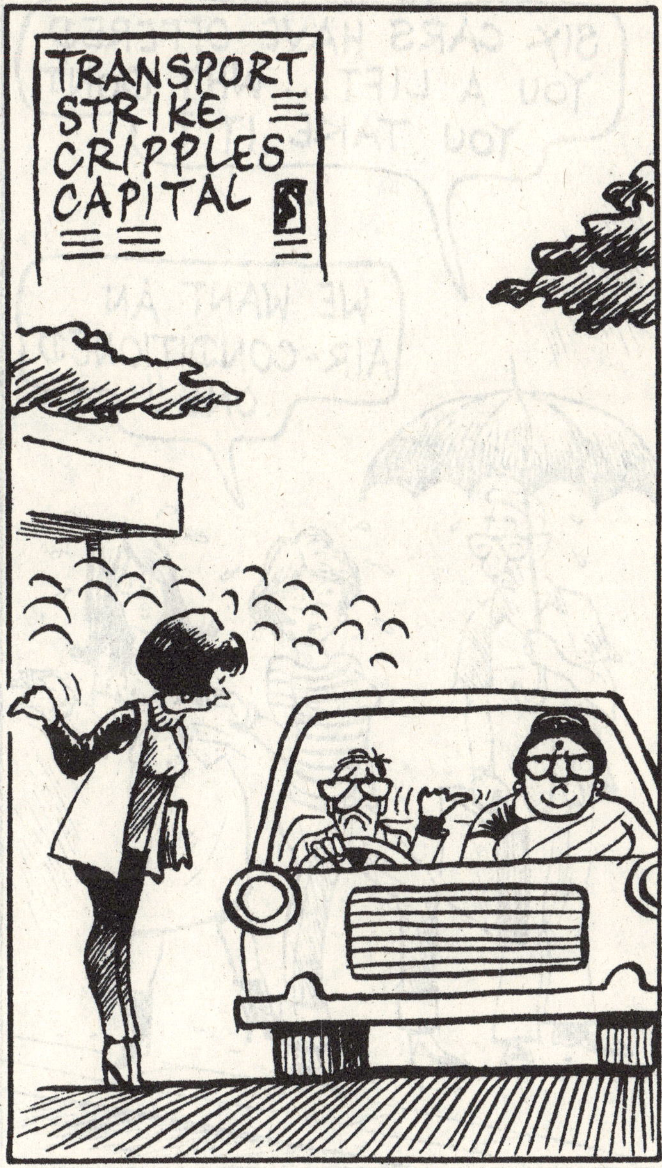
TRANSPORT STRIKE CRIPPLES CAPITAL

"THAT YOU, DEAR..?"

"FOR YOU, DARLING — IT'S YOUR WIFE!"

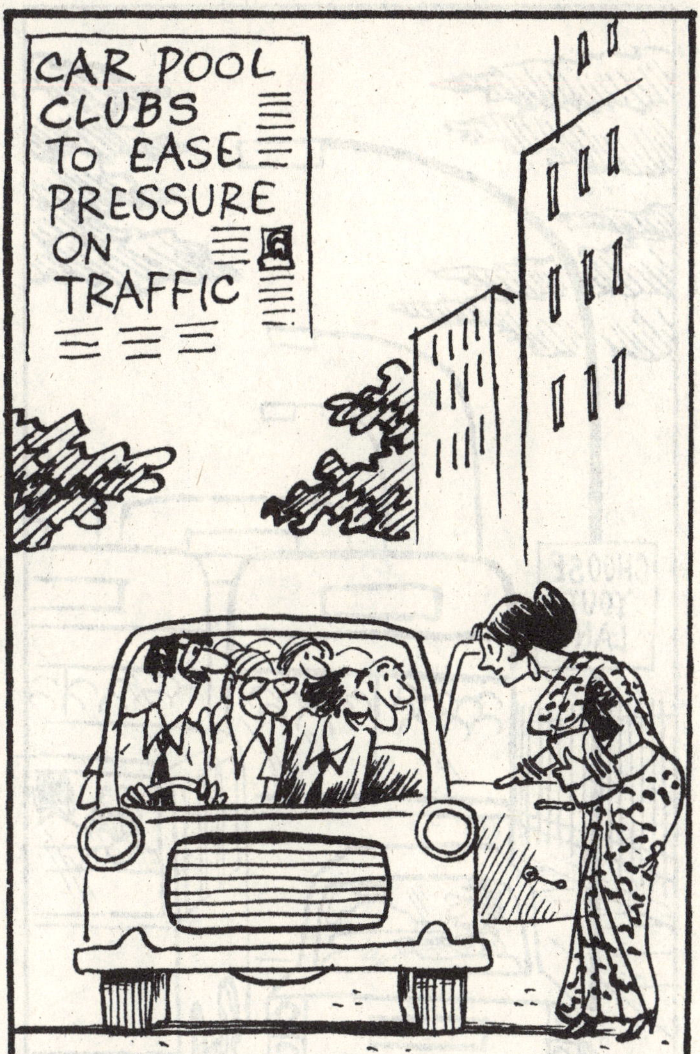
CAR POOL CLUBS TO EASE PRESSURE ON TRAFFIC

"NO PROBLEM, MISS... WE DON'T MIND A TIGHT SQUEEZE!"

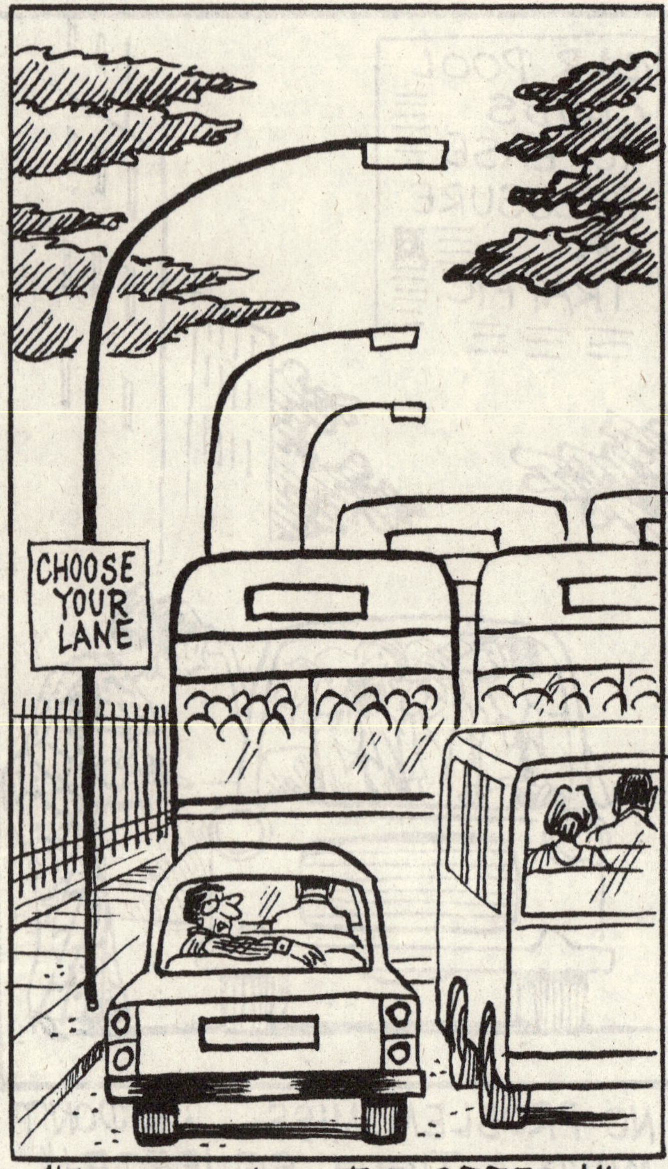
CHOOSE YOUR LANE

"THANKS FOR THE OFFER!"

"GREEN?? WHICH DELHI IS THAT?!"

"FANTASTIC INDIAN INVENTION, SIR..
RUNS ON NIMBU PANI!"

"CHEERS!"

"THERE SHOULD BE THREE FARES—
SEATING, STANDING AND HANGING!"

"HELLO, NATIONAL GALLERY OF MODERN ART..?"

"NOT THESE, YOU IDIOT— NOT THE VVIP CARS!"

"IF THEY'RE 'SERVANTS OF THE PEOPLE' WHY MUST THEY **HIDE** FROM THE PEOPLE..?!"

"WE DON'T NEED AN 'ACT'—
WE NEED 'ACTION'!!"

"MOSQUITOES? NO PROBLEM..
MY HUSBAND TAKES CARE
OF THEM!"

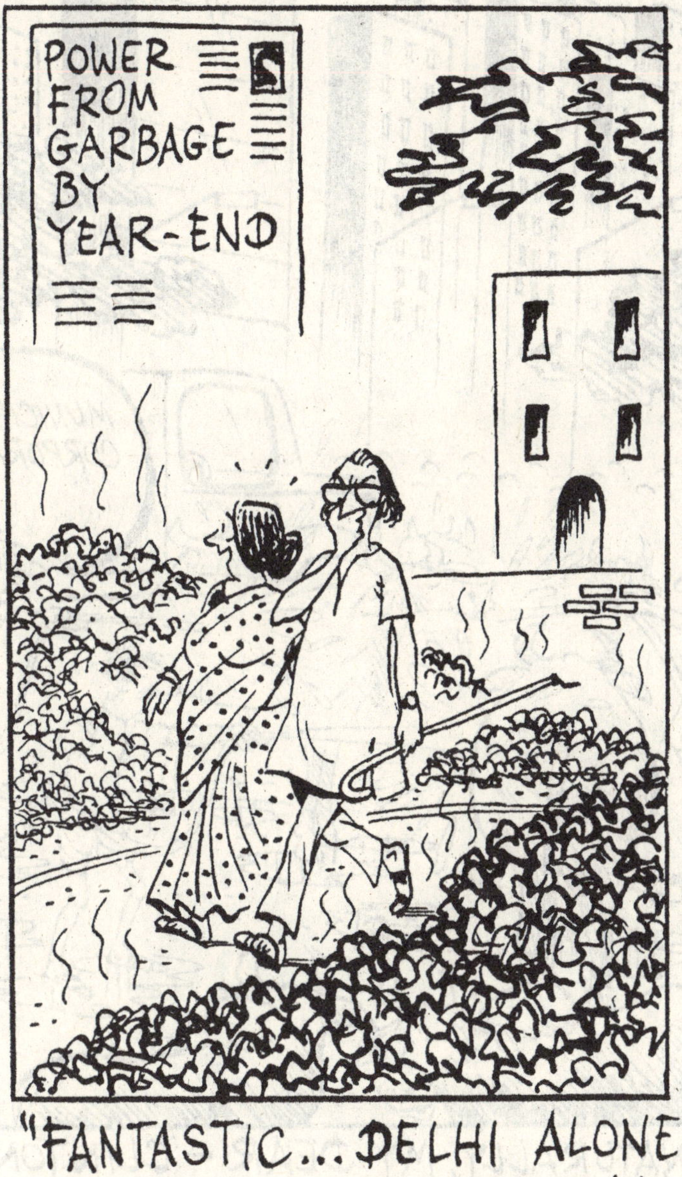
POWER FROM GARBAGE BY YEAR-END

"FANTASTIC... DELHI ALONE COULD FEED INDIA!"

"NATURALLY, MY DEAR – CLINTON DOESN'T COME EVERY DAY!"

"IT WAS RUNNING BEAUTIFULLY TILL YESTERDAY.. THEN WE PLAYED 'RUK, RUK, RUK'.. AND IT STOPPED!"

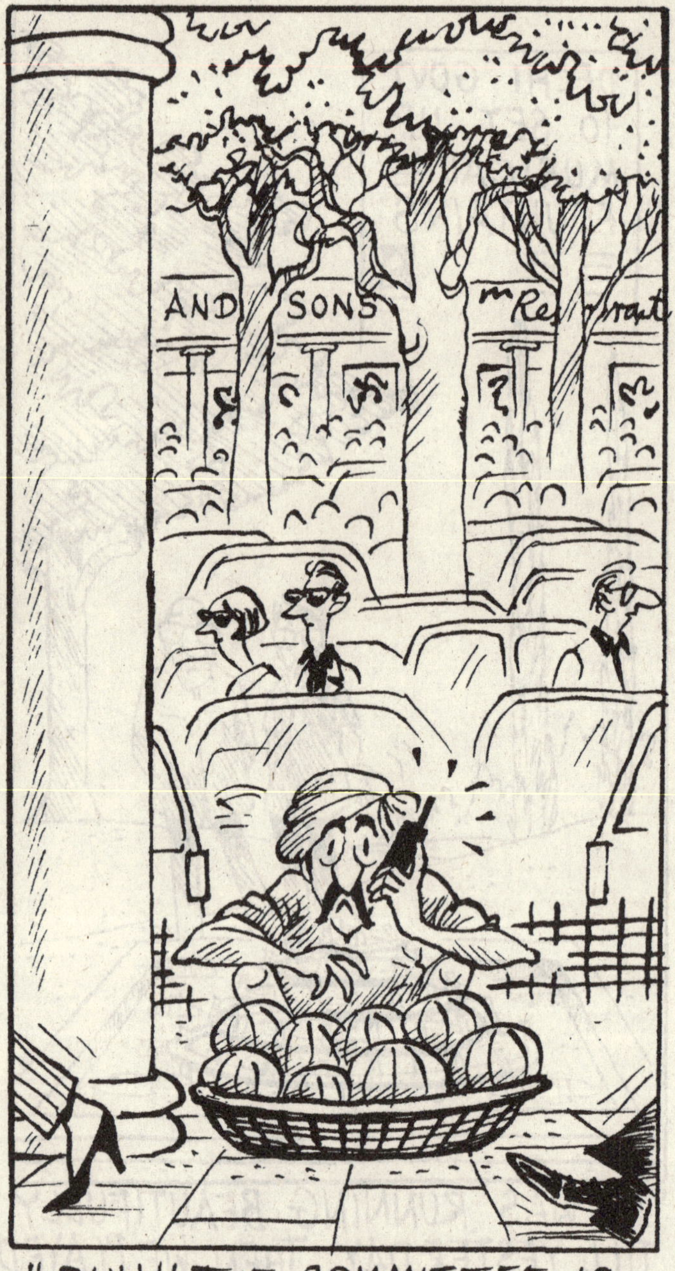
AND SONS
Re...rant

"RUN!! THE COMMITTEE IS COMING!!"

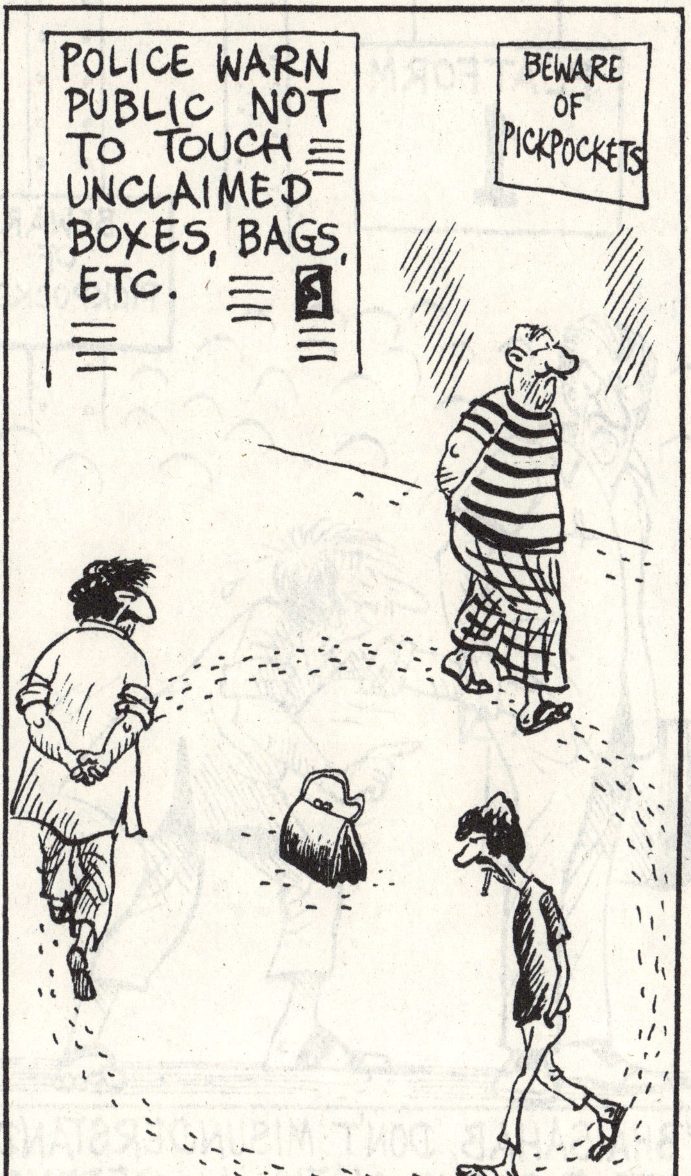
POLICE WARN PUBLIC NOT TO TOUCH UNCLAIMED BOXES, BAGS, ETC.
BEWARE OF PICKPOCKETS

"BHAISAHAB, DON'T MISUNDERSTAND..
IT'S FOR THE NATIONAL DEFENCE
FUND!"

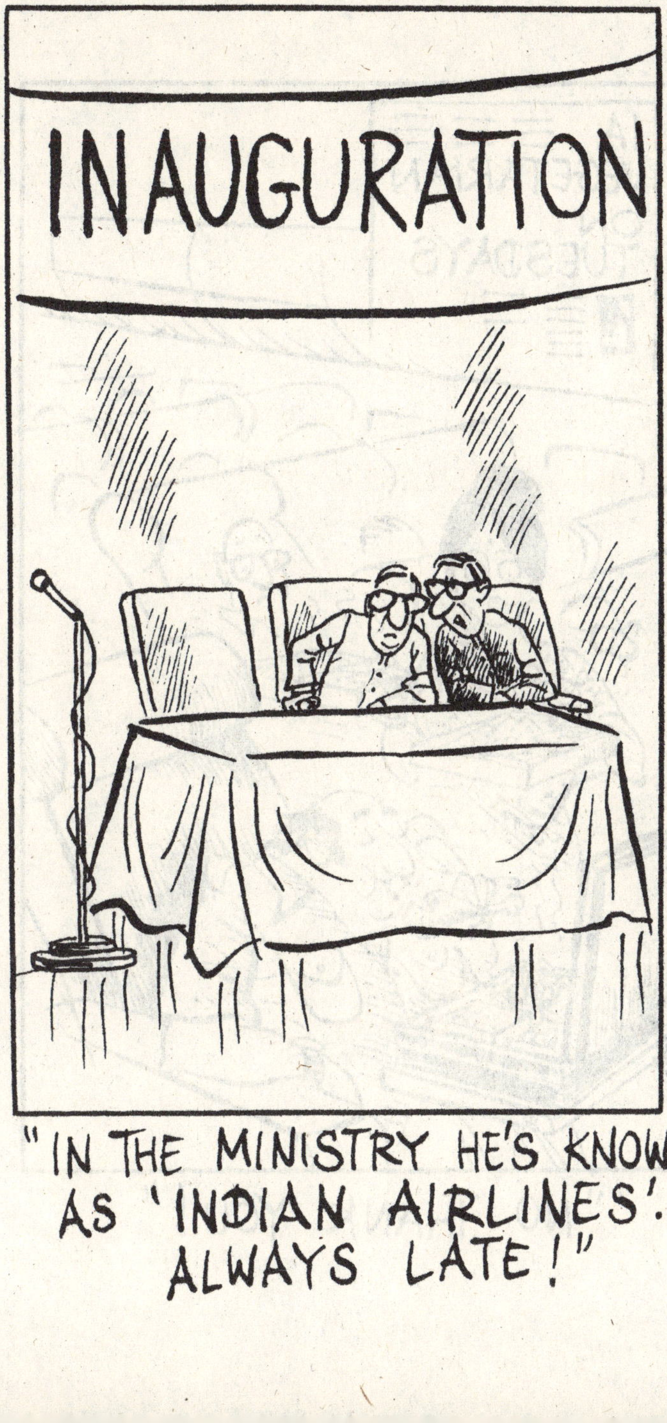
INAUGURATION

"IN THE MINISTRY HE'S KNOWN AS 'INDIAN AIRLINES'... ALWAYS LATE!"

"NO THANK YOU!"

"SORRY, SIR—VERY SHORT FLIGHT—NO TIME FOR CUPS!"

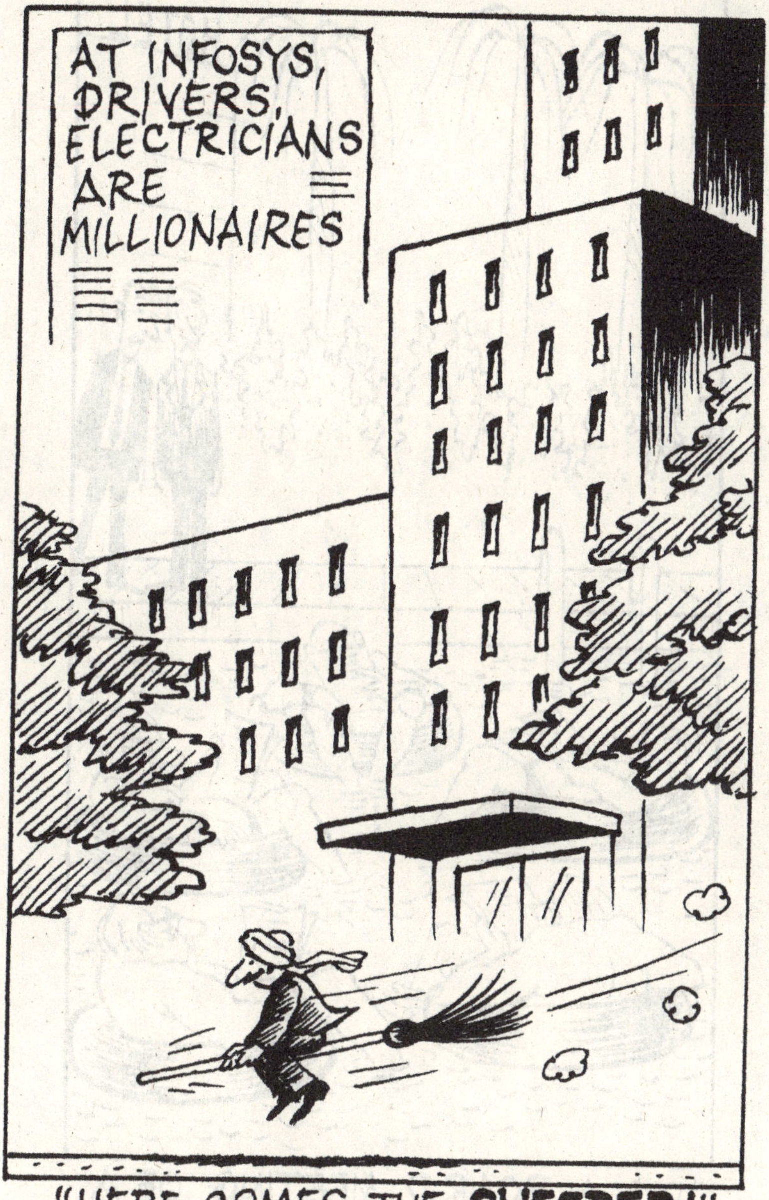
AT INFOSYS, DRIVERS, ELECTRICIANS ARE MILLIONAIRES

"HERE COMES THE **SWEEPER!**"

"IT'S A BOARD MEETING OF A TYRE COMPANY...!"

"I'LL JOIN YOU IN A FEW MINUTES, DEAR — AS SOON AS I FINISH MY DRINK!"

"CONTINENTAL? WHICH CONTINENT?!"

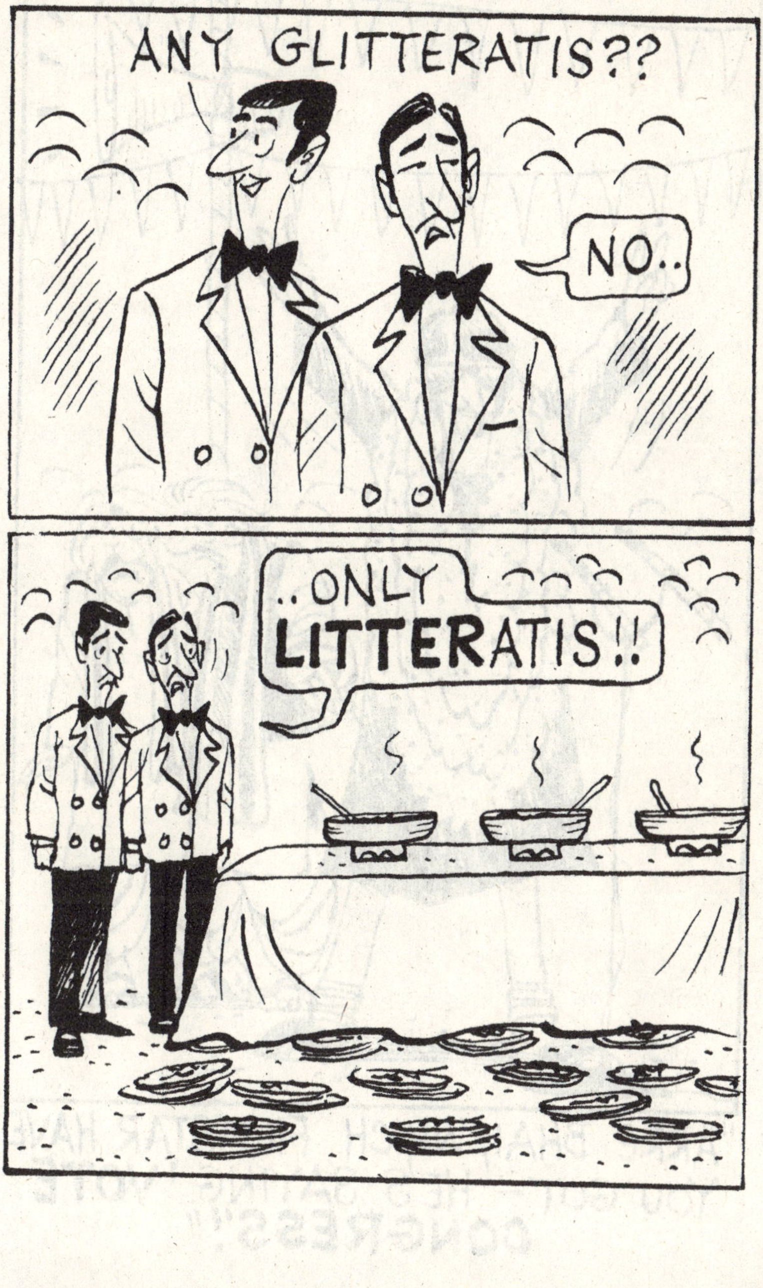
ANY GLITTERATIS??
NO..
..ONLY LITTERATIS!!

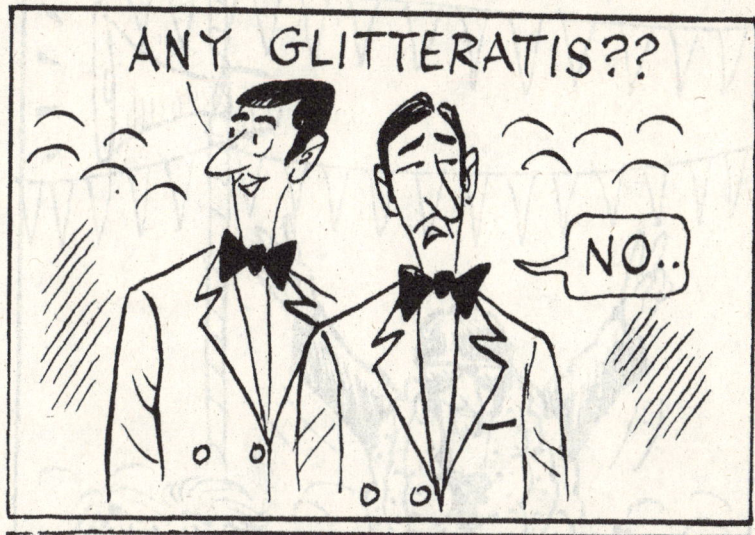

"ARRE BHAI, WHICH FILMSTAR HAVE YOU GOT— HE'S SAYING 'VOTE CONGRESS'!"

"VOTE BJP!"

"WHO'S FUNDING HIS CAMPAIGN—
CHANNEL [V] ?!"

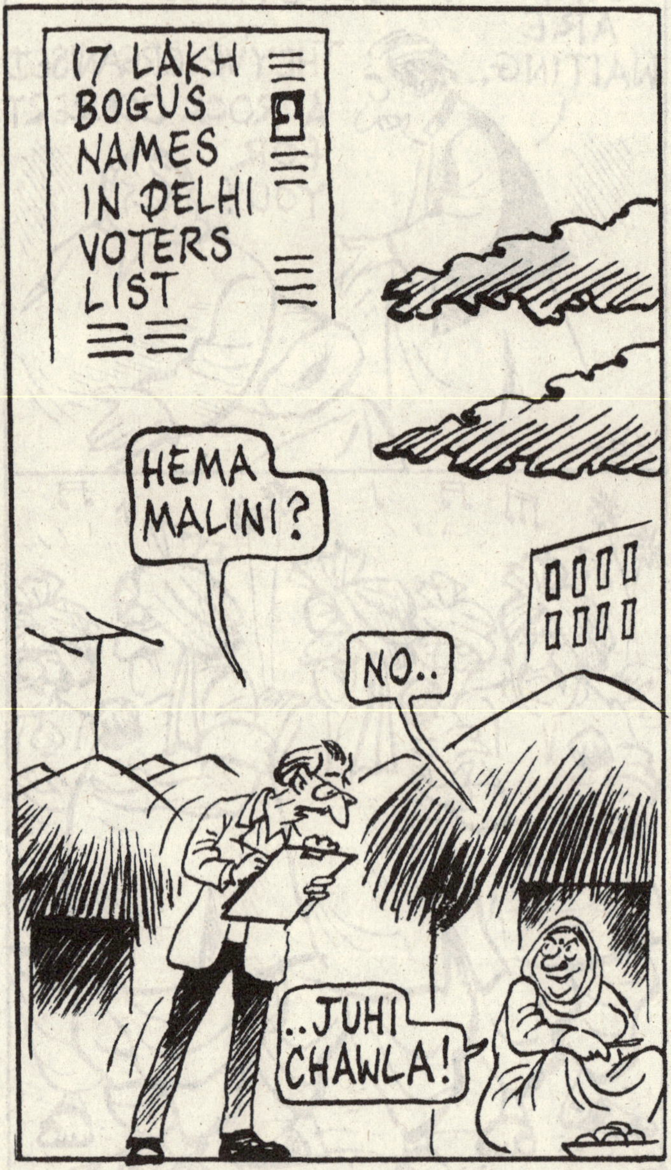

17 LAKH BOGUS NAMES IN DELHI VOTERS LIST
HEMA MALINI?
NO..
..JUHI CHAWLA!

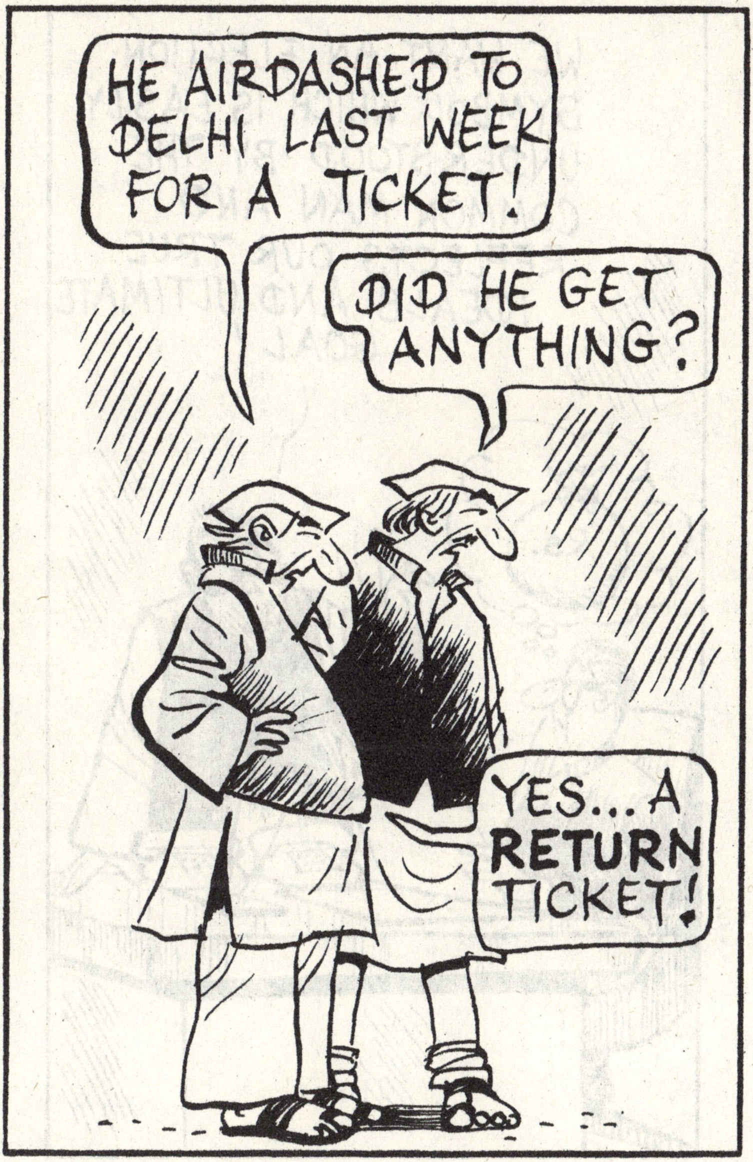
HE AIRDASHED TO DELHI LAST WEEK FOR A TICKET!
DID HE GET ANYTHING?
YES... A **RETURN** TICKET!

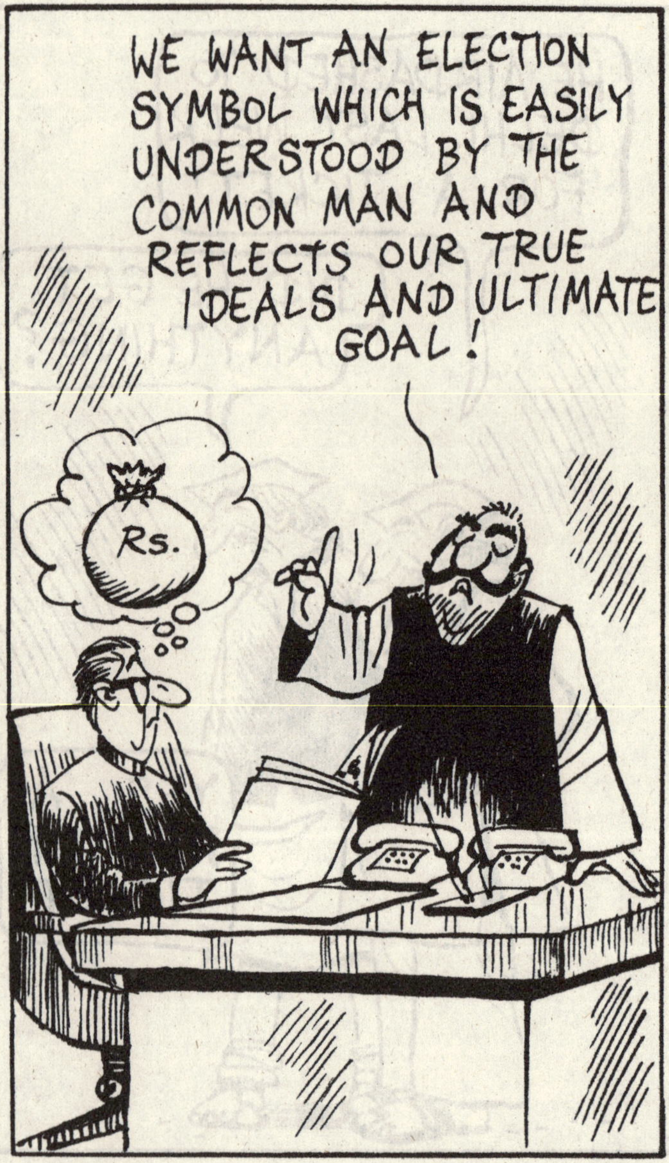
WE WANT AN ELECTION SYMBOL WHICH IS EASILY UNDERSTOOD BY THE COMMON MAN AND REFLECTS OUR TRUE IDEALS AND ULTIMATE GOAL!
Rs.

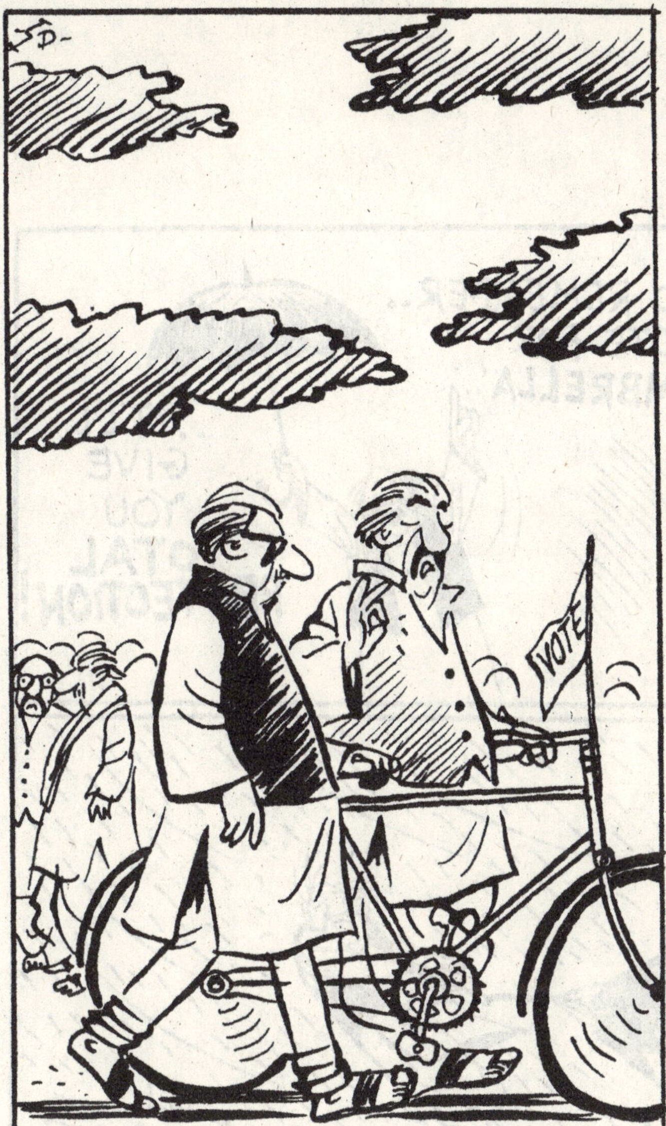
VOTE

"FOR OUR CONSTITUENCY HE'S PERFECT! HIS FATHER'S A THAKUR, MOTHER'S A BRAHMIN AND WIFE'S A HARIJAN..!"

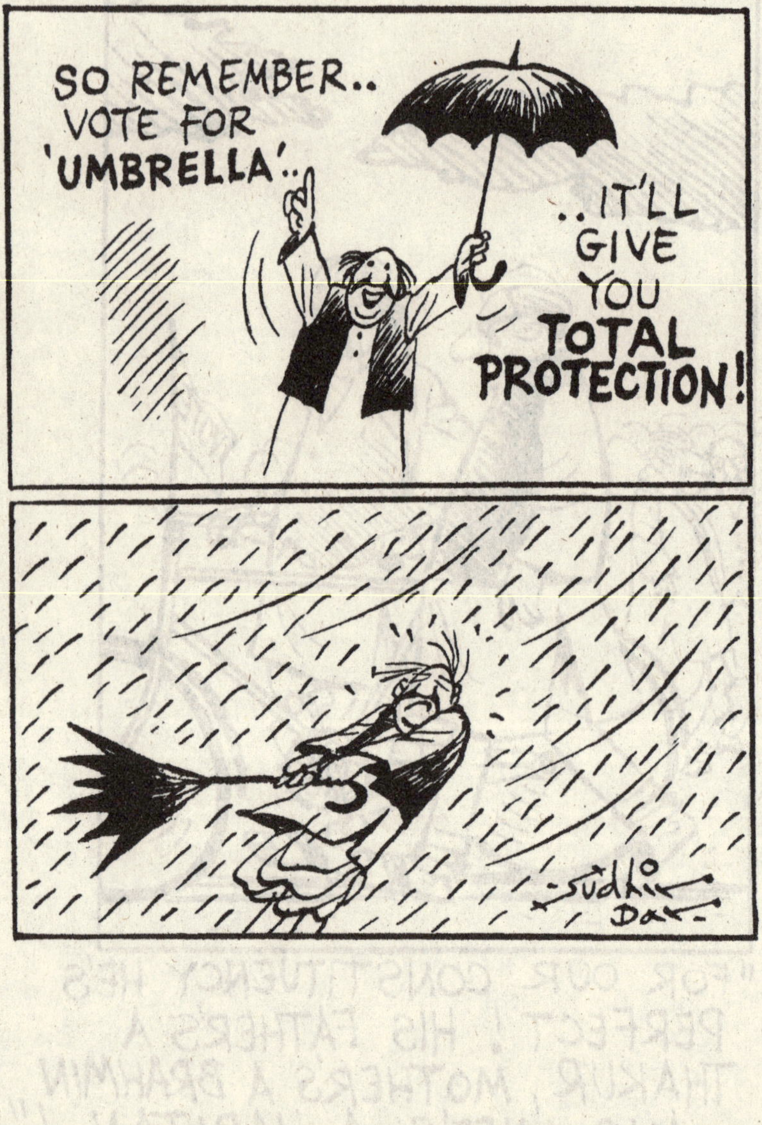
SO REMEMBER.. VOTE FOR 'UMBRELLA'..
..IT'LL GIVE YOU TOTAL PROTECTION!
Sudhir Dar

"BHAISAAB... **EVERY** VOTE COUNTS!"

"WE BELIEVE YOU'RE LOOKING FOR LIKE-MINDED PARTIES..!"

"THE BRITISH HAVE SUCH A CIVILIZED WAY OF EXPRESSING THINGS..!"

"NOW IS THE TIME FOR ALL GOOD **FANATICS** TO COME TO THE AID OF THE PARTY..!"

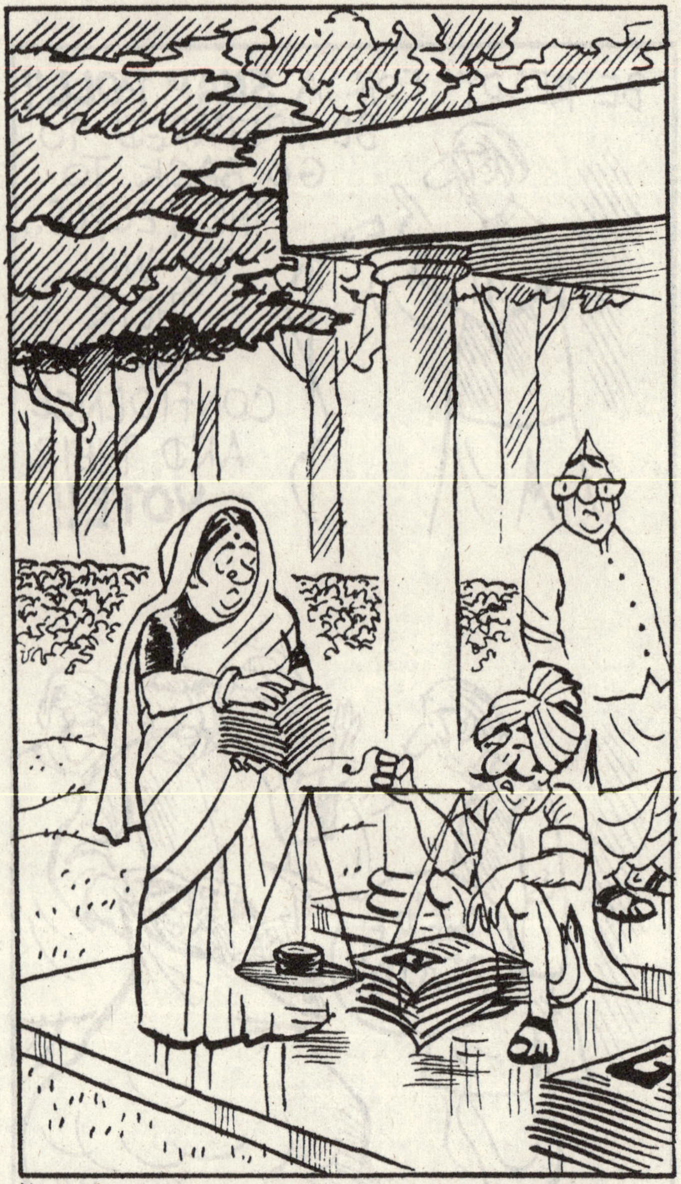

"MANIFESTOS?! NO THANKS – I ONLY BUY PAPER THAT'S WORTH SOMETHING!"

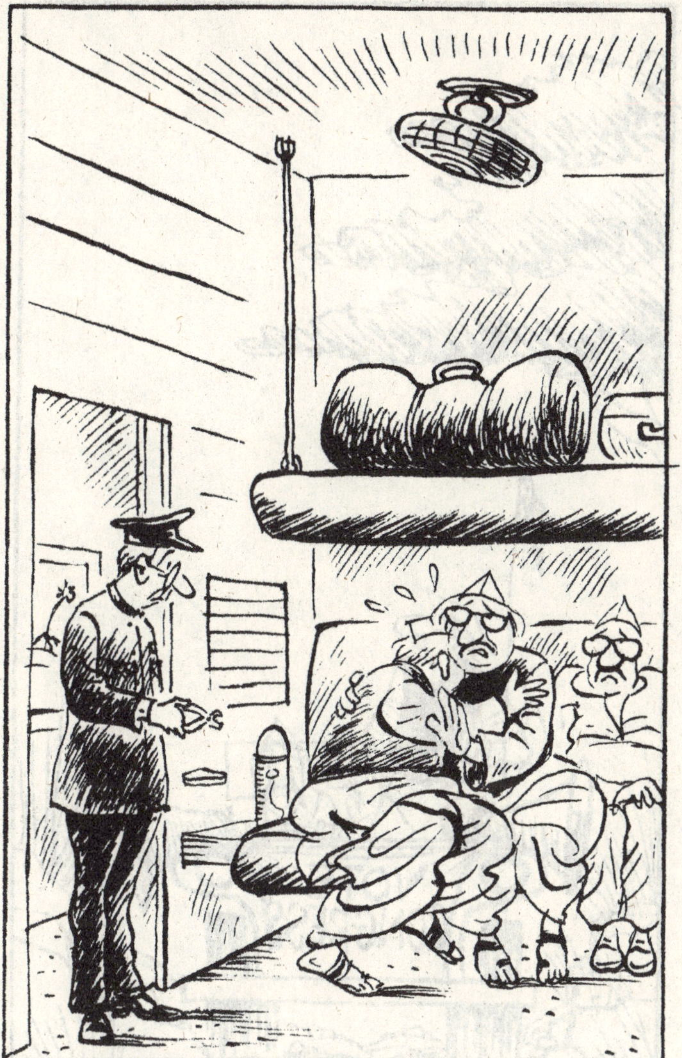

"TICKET! DON'T MENTION IT, PLEASE — IT'S A VERY SENSITIVE SUBJECT!"

"OH YES, THIS IS MY CONSTITUENCY, ALL RIGHT...!"

"TOUGH CONSTITUENCY... WOMEN'S VOTE IS VITAL!"

"LAST TIME HE WON BY A LANDSLIDE—
HIS OPPONENT GOT BURIED UNDER
FALLING ROCKS!"

"HE CAME AS A GREAT MESSIAH..
BUT HE MADE A GREAT MESS!"

"RELAX! WE'VE JUST COME TO ENSURE A FREE, FAIR AND PEACEFUL POLL... IN FAVOUR OF **OUR** CANDIDATE!"

"EXCEPT FOR A FEW CASES OF ARSON, MURDER, BOMB ATTACKS, VIOLENCE AND RIOTING, POLLING WAS VERY PEACEFUL..!"

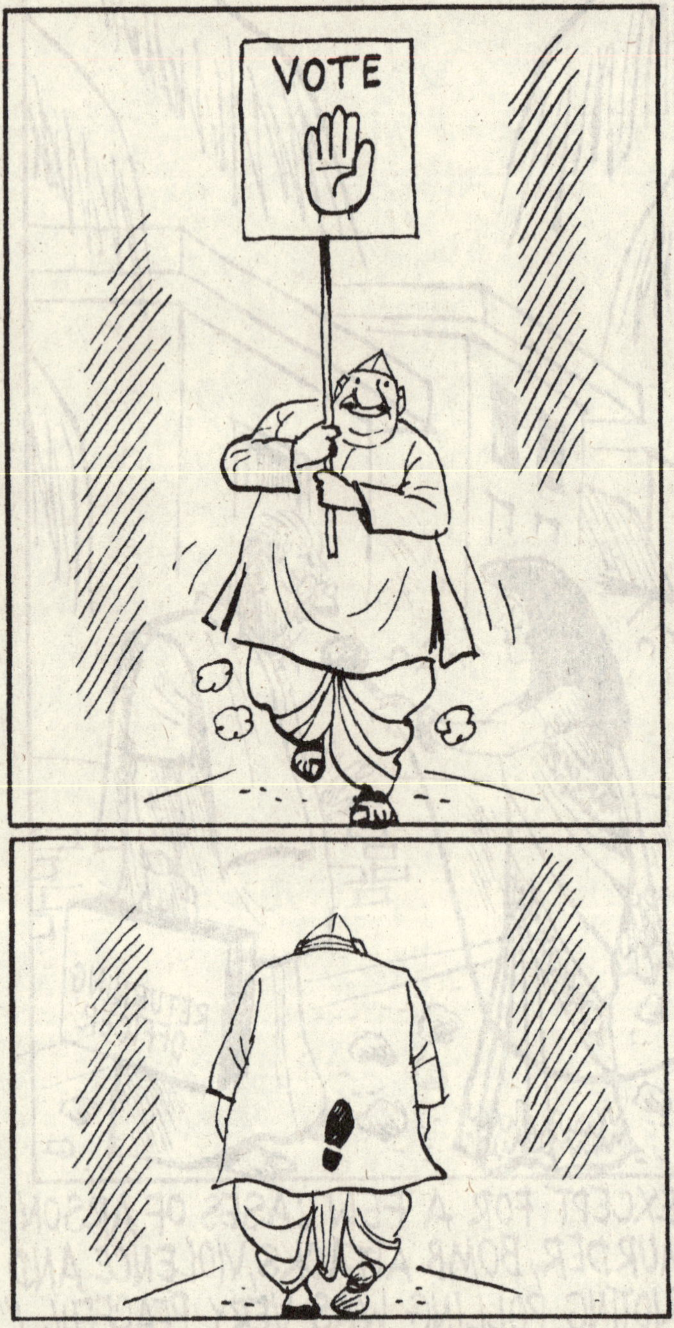
VOTE

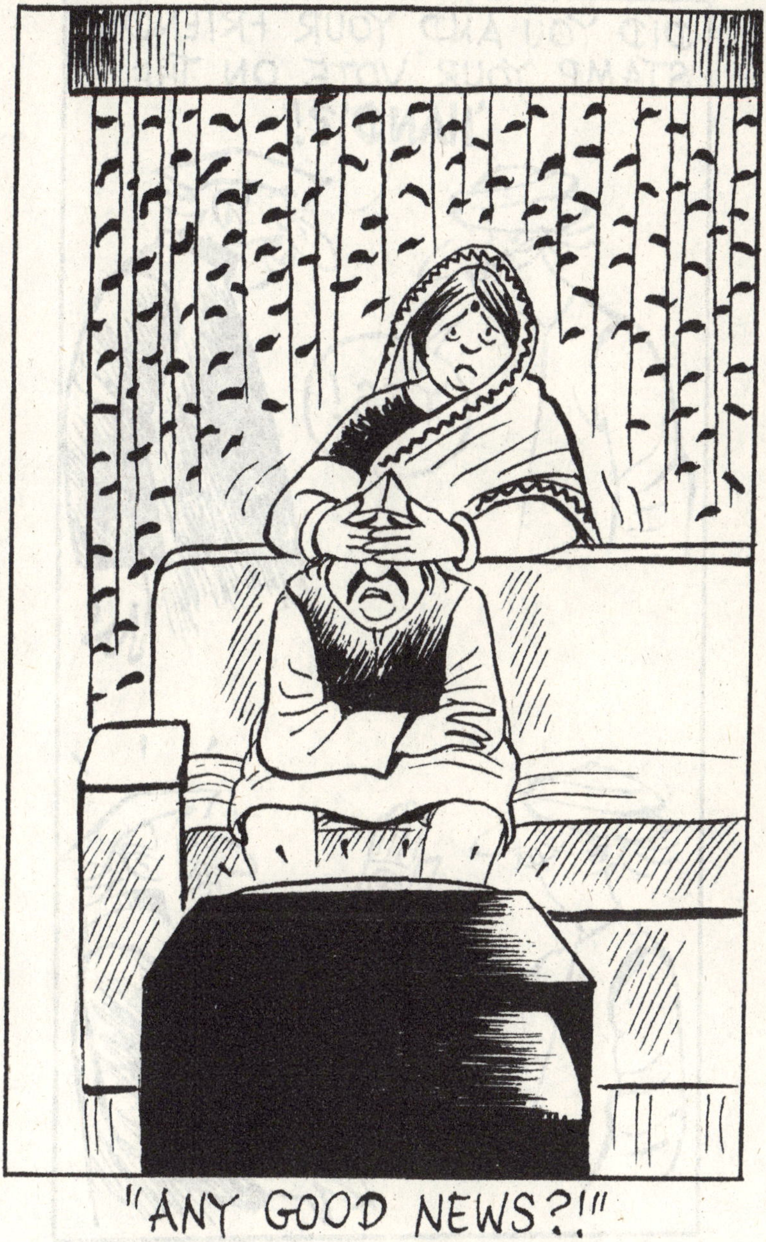

"ANY GOOD NEWS?!"

"I TOLD HIM THAT HE WOULD GO FAR... BUT HE MUSTN'T GO TOO FAR!"

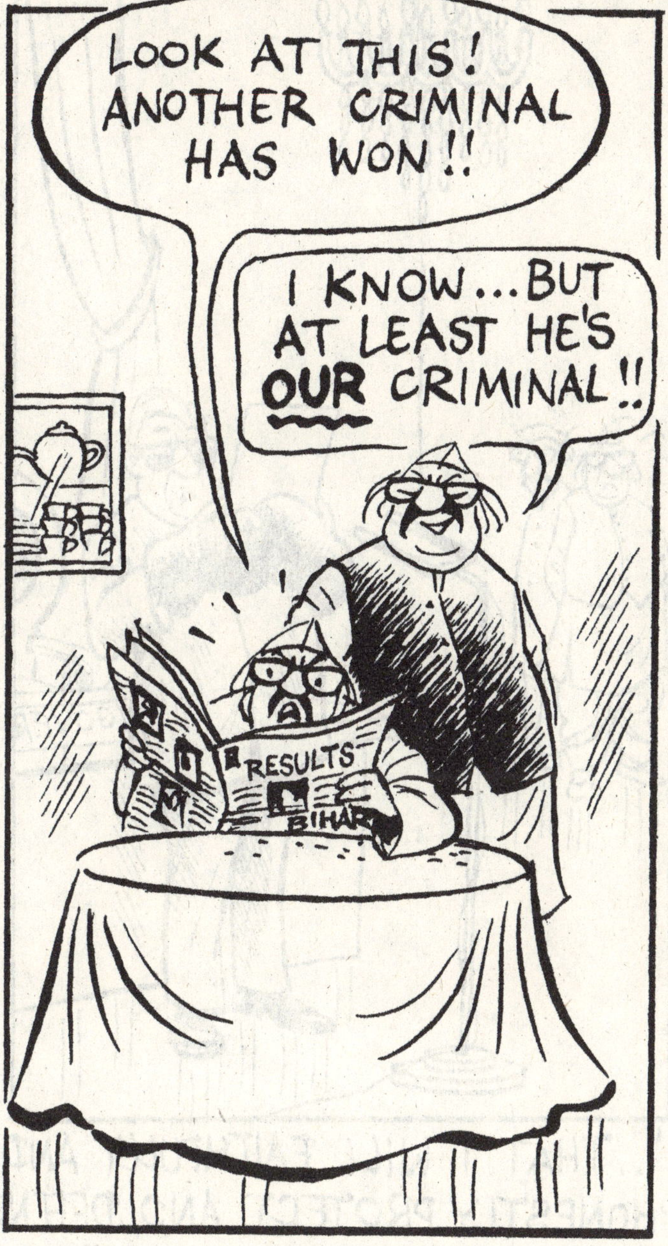

LOOK AT THIS! ANOTHER CRIMINAL HAS WON!!
I KNOW...BUT AT LEAST HE'S OUR CRIMINAL!!
RESULTS
BIHAR

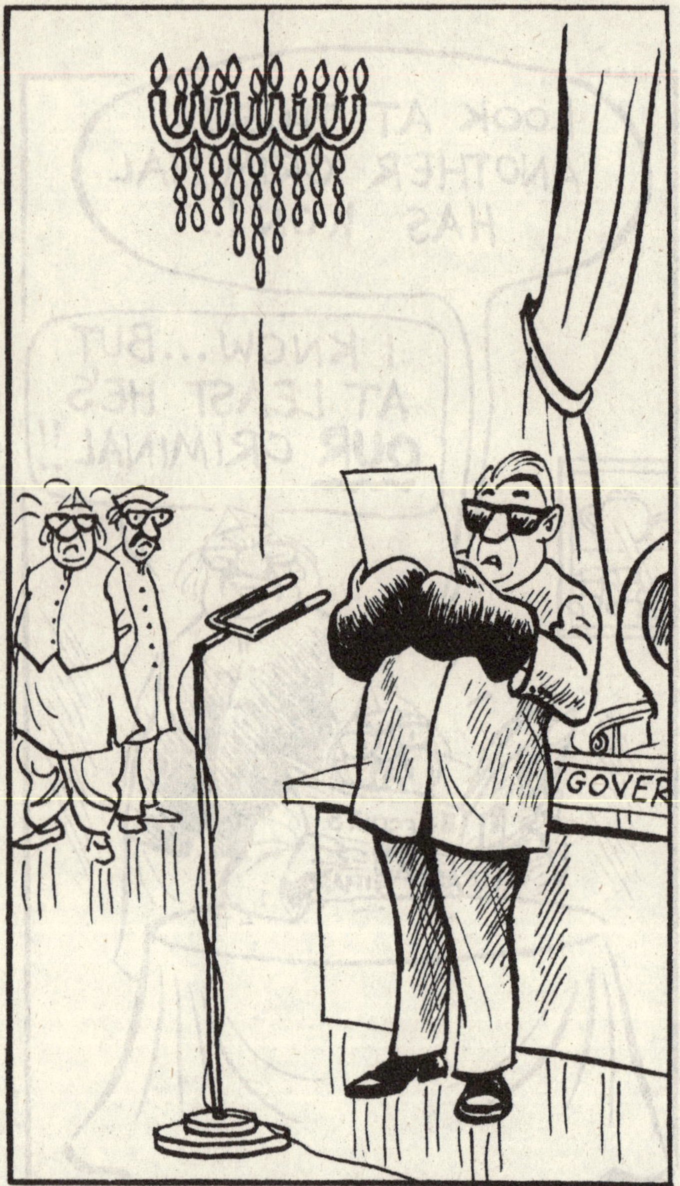
GOVER

"..THAT I WILL FAITHFULLY AND HONESTLY PROTECT AND DEFEND THE CONSTITUTION."

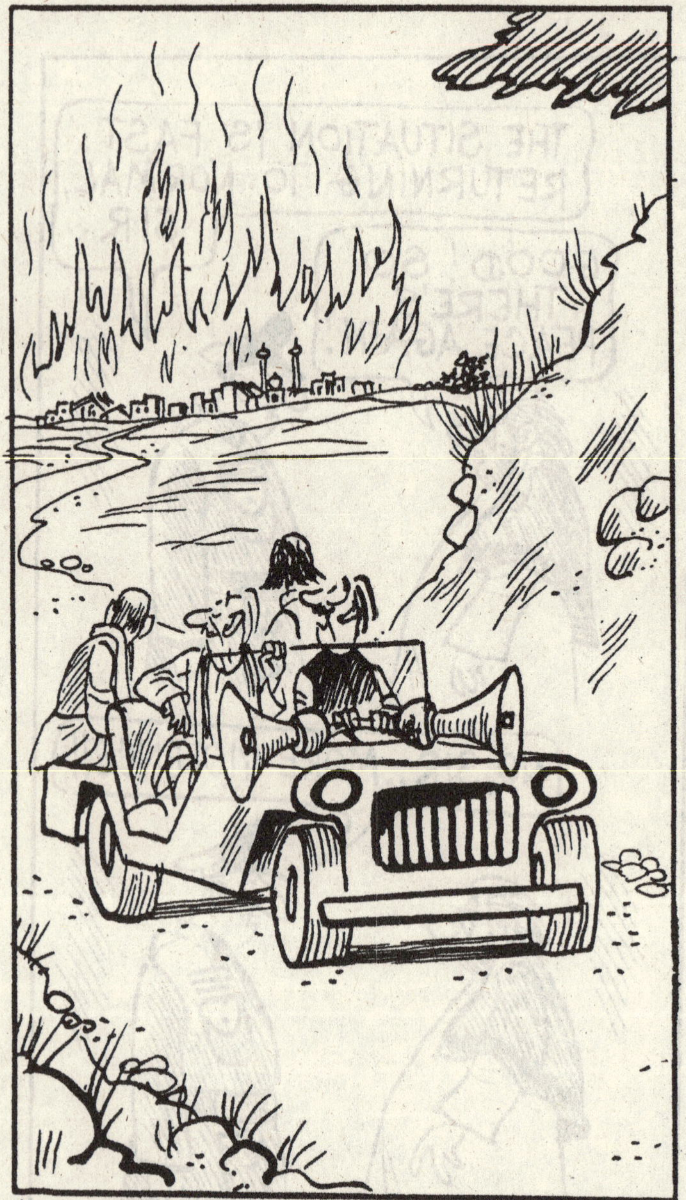

"THERE YOU ARE – YOUR VISIT WAS HIGHLY SUCCESSFUL!"

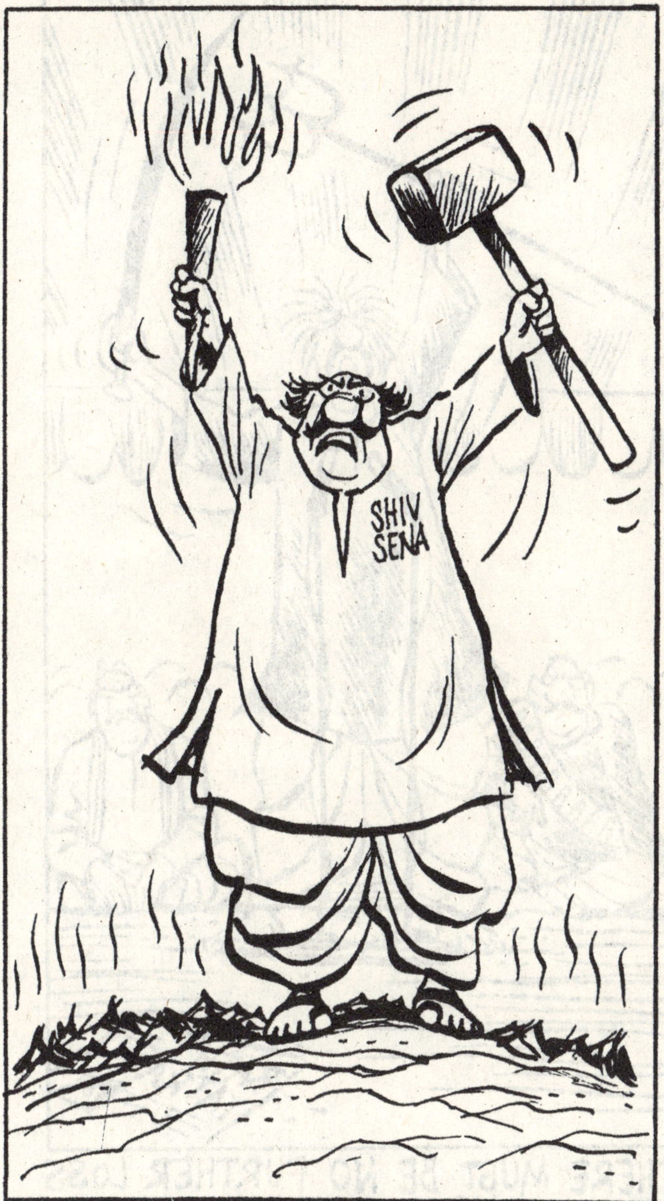
SHIV
SENA

"ANYTHING **BABAR** CAN DO, **WE** CAN DO **BETTER!!**"

"THERE MUST BE NO FURTHER LOSS OF LIVES! PEACE, HARMONY AND SANITY MUST BE RESTORED! NOTHING MUST COME IN THE WAY!!"

"BAN OR NO BAN, BJP ASSURES YOU THAT ALL FUTURE DEMOLITIONS WILL BE DONE IN A DISCIPLINED, PEACEFUL MANNER!"

"WE'VE GOT IRREFUTABLE EVIDENCE THAT ONCE THERE WAS A TEMPLE HERE..!"

"CUT OUT THIS SWADESHI VS. VIDESHI CAMPAIGN — YOU'RE HURTING MY FEELINGS, DAD!"

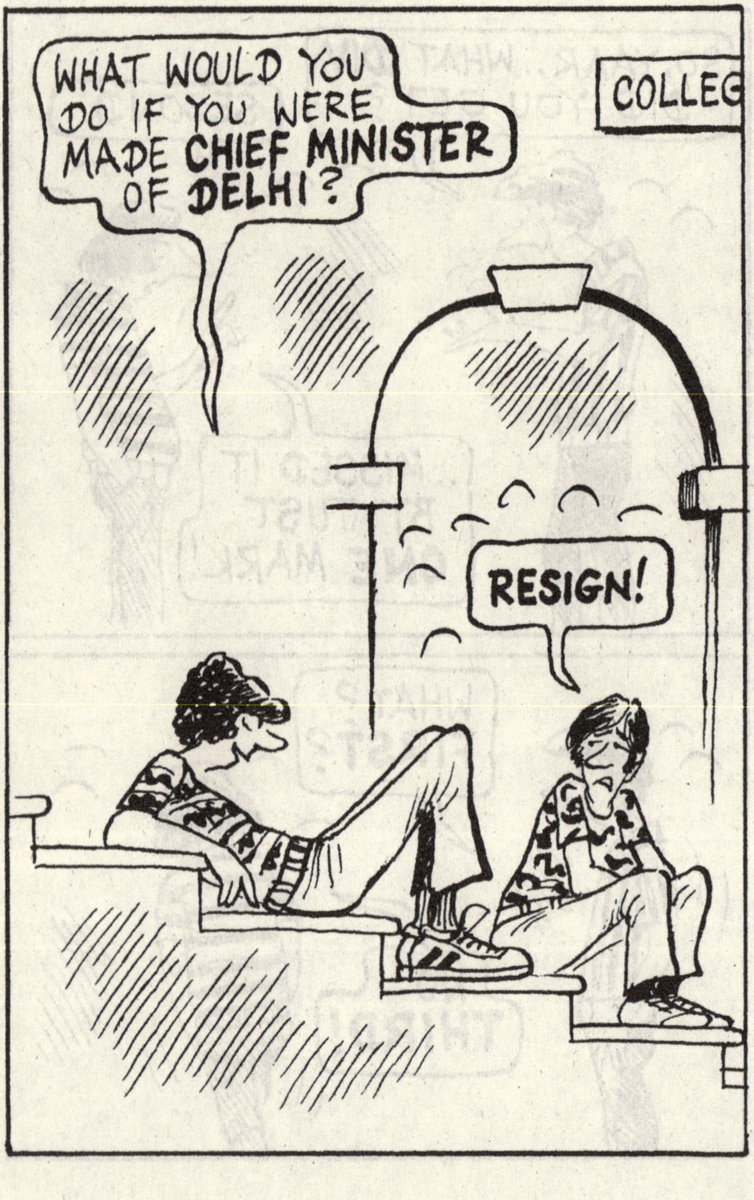
WHAT WOULD YOU DO IF YOU WERE MADE CHIEF MINISTER OF DELHI?
COLLEG
RESIGN!

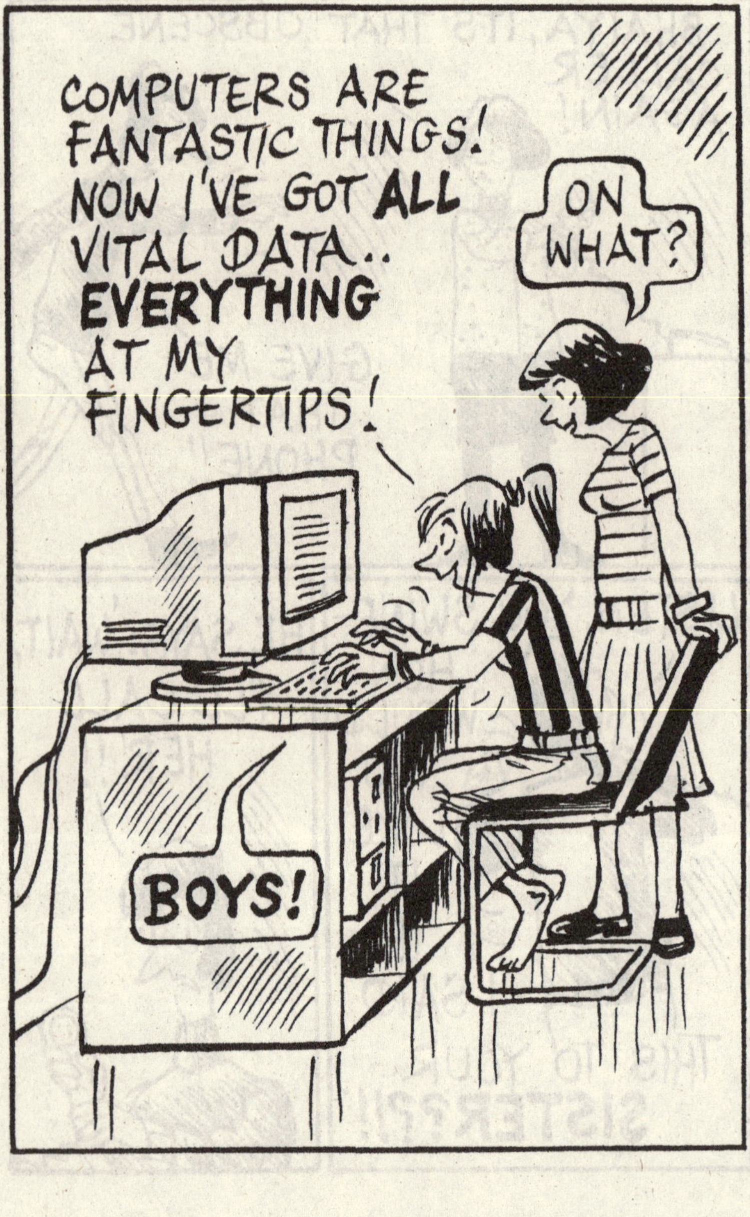
COMPUTERS ARE FANTASTIC THINGS! NOW I'VE GOT **ALL** VITAL DATA.. **EVERYTHING** AT MY FINGERTIPS!
ON WHAT?
BOYS!

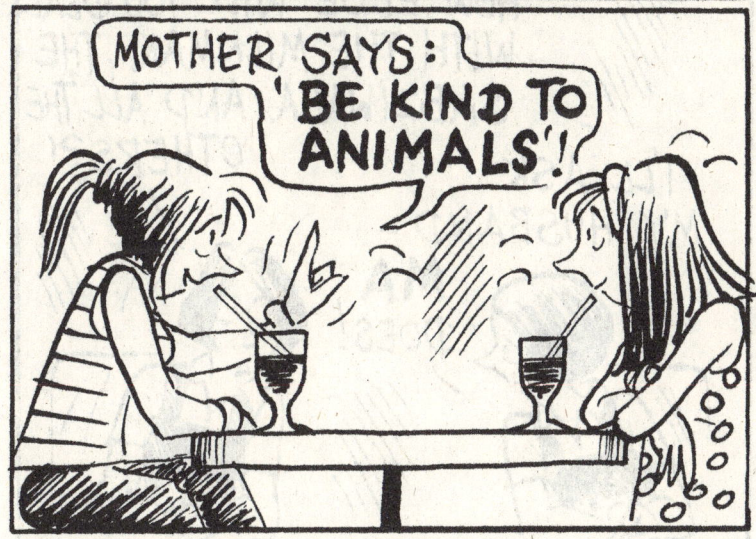

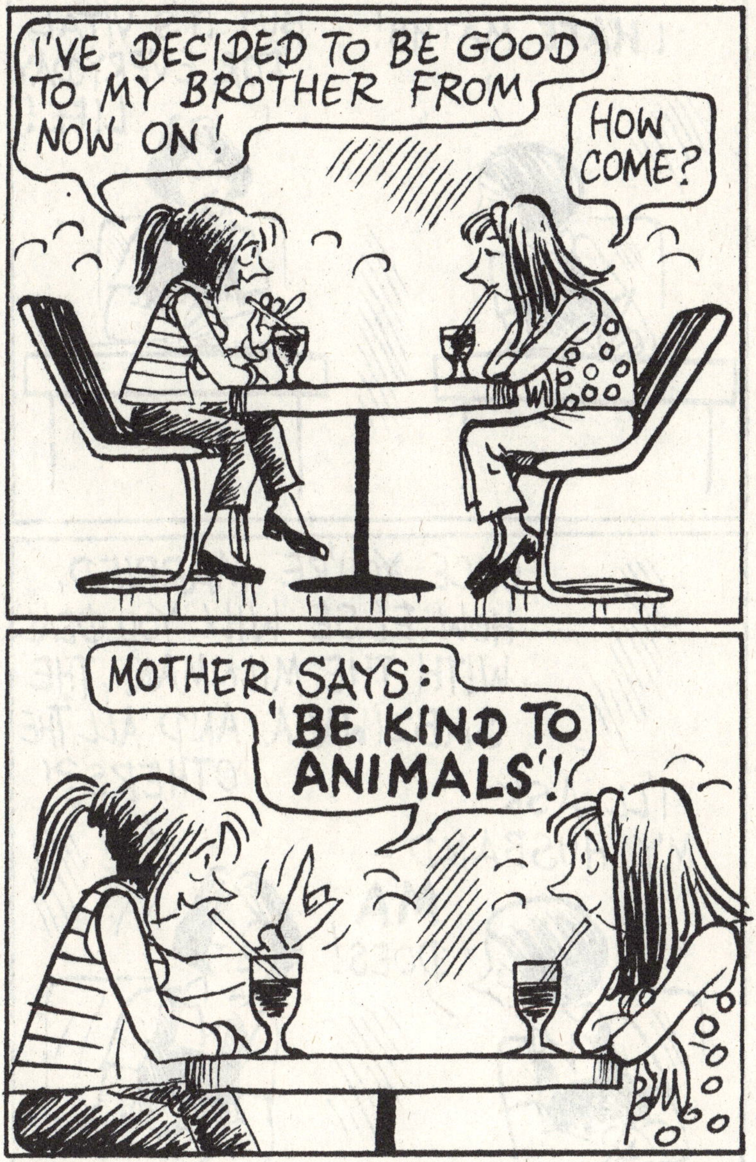
I'VE DECIDED TO BE GOOD TO MY BROTHER FROM NOW ON!
HOW COME?
MOTHER SAYS: 'BE KIND TO ANIMALS'!

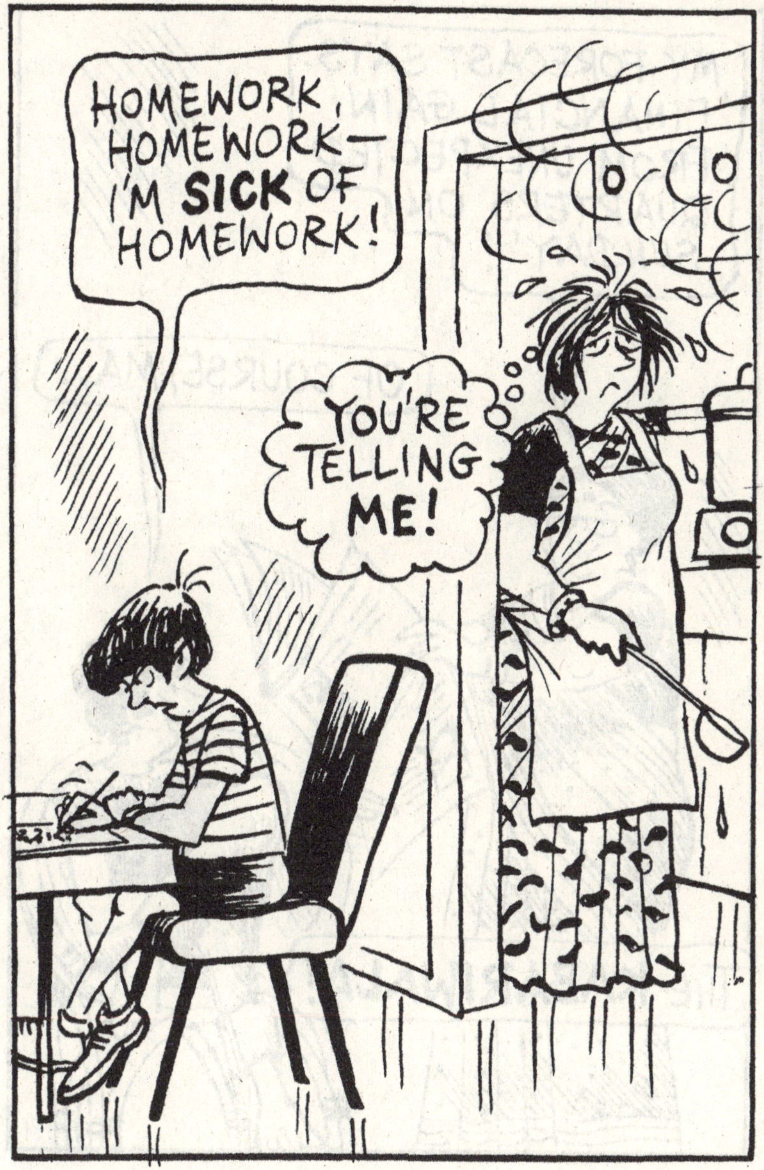
HOMEWORK, HOMEWORK— I'M **SICK** OF HOMEWORK!
YOU'RE TELLING **ME**!

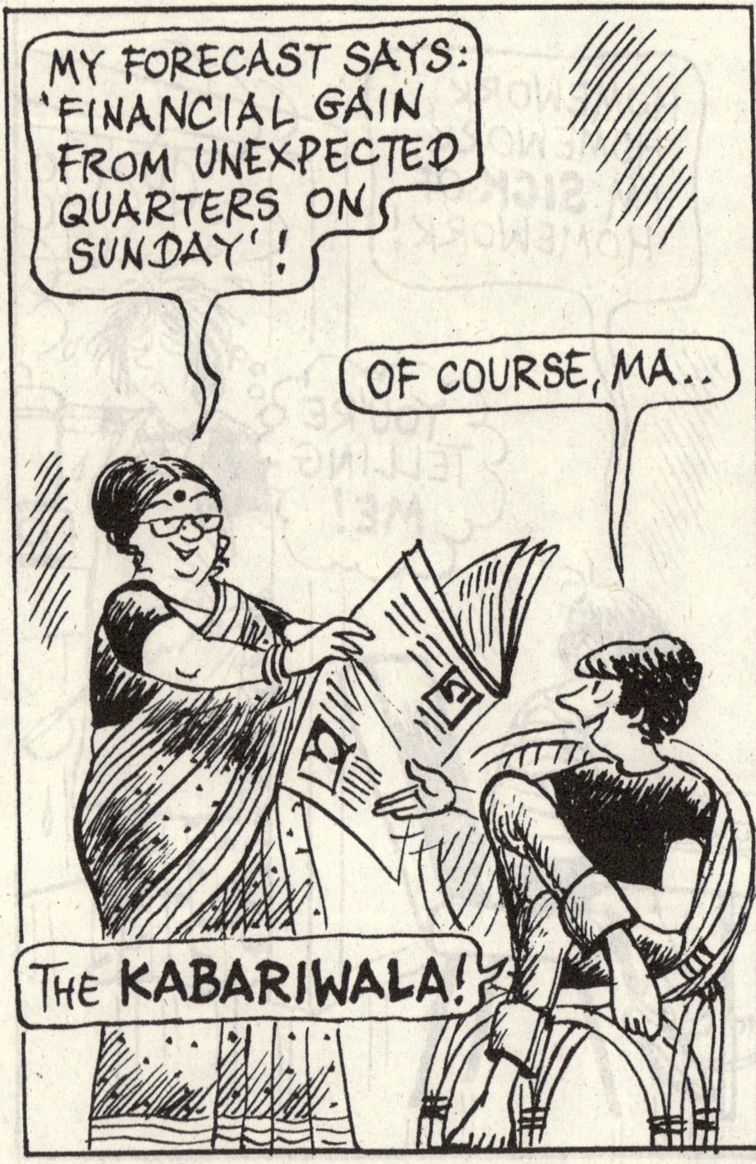
MY FORECAST SAYS: 'FINANCIAL GAIN FROM UNEXPECTED QUARTERS ON SUNDAY'!
OF COURSE, MA..
THE **KABARIWALA**!

"SHE BEATS OPRAH WINFREY...THAT TALK SHOW IS OVER IN AN **HOUR!**"

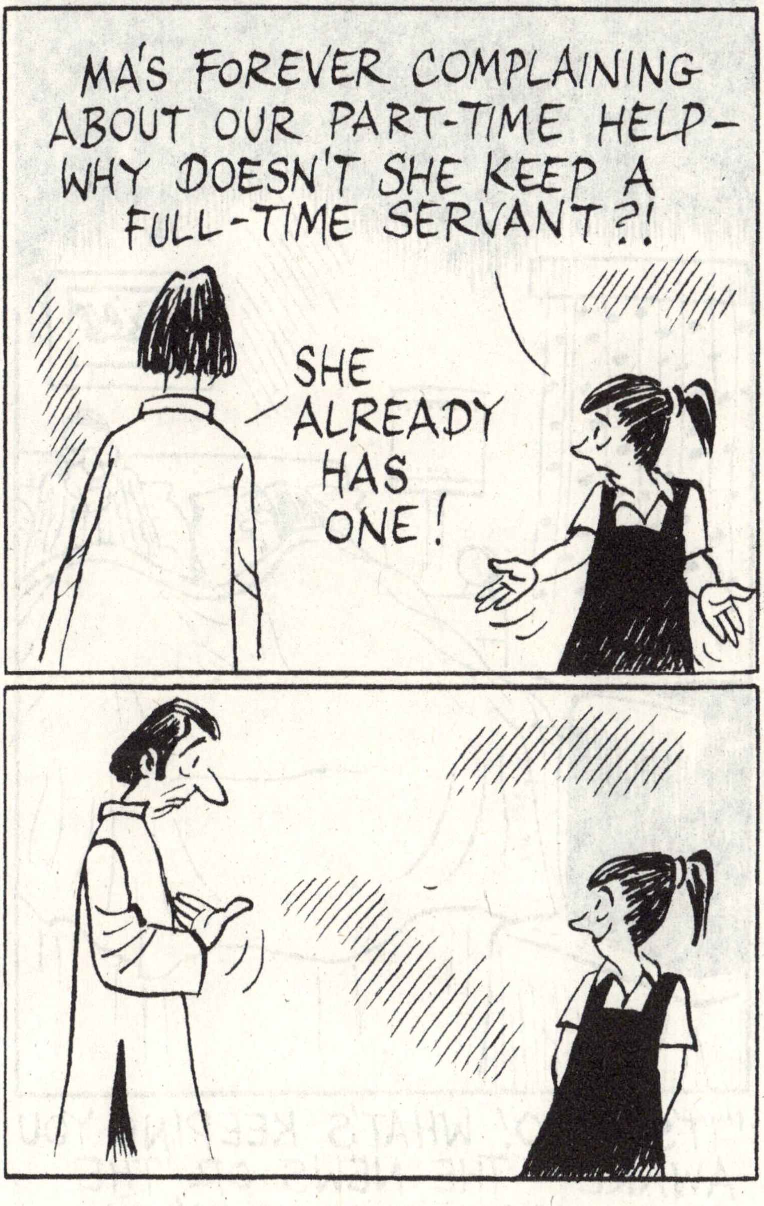
MA'S FOREVER COMPLAINING ABOUT OUR PART-TIME HELP- WHY DOESN'T SHE KEEP A FULL-TIME SERVANT?!
SHE ALREADY HAS ONE!

"IT'S 11:30! WHAT'S KEEPING YOU AWAKE — THE NEWS OR THE NEWSREADER?!"

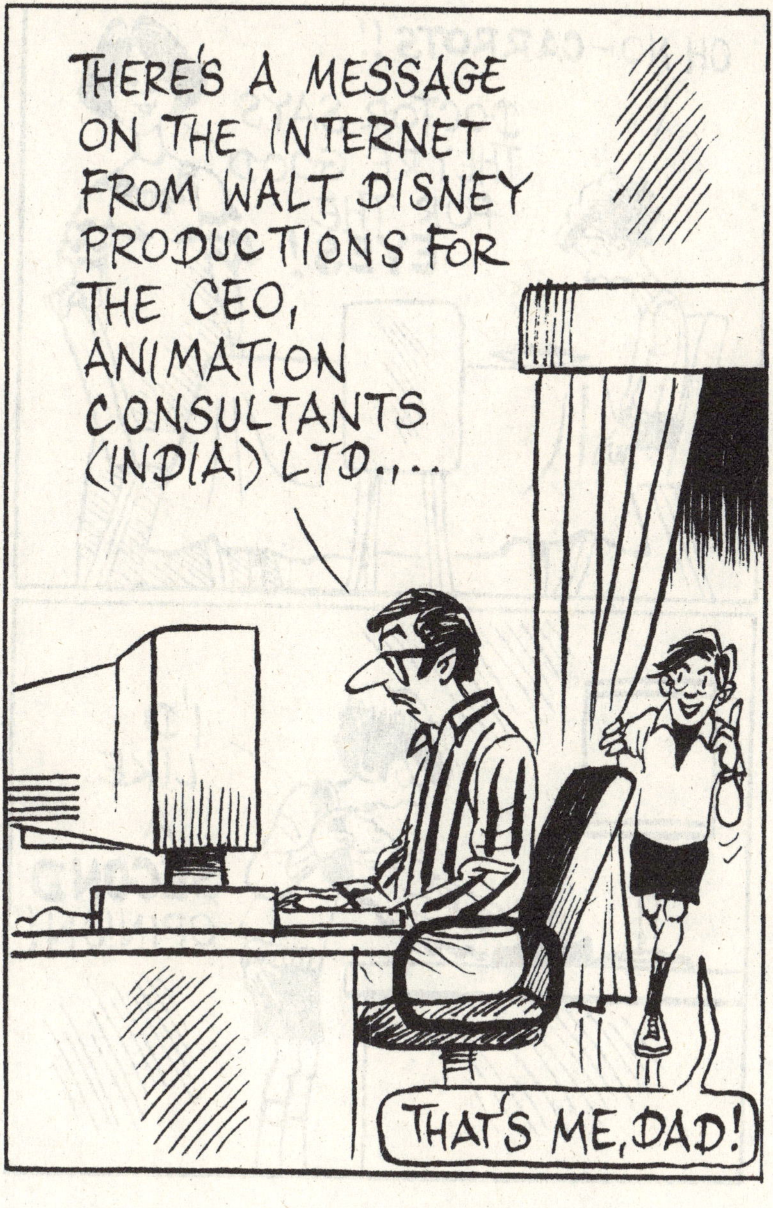
THERE'S A MESSAGE ON THE INTERNET FROM WALT DISNEY PRODUCTIONS FOR THE CEO, ANIMATION CONSULTANTS (INDIA) LTD.,..
THAT'S ME, DAD!

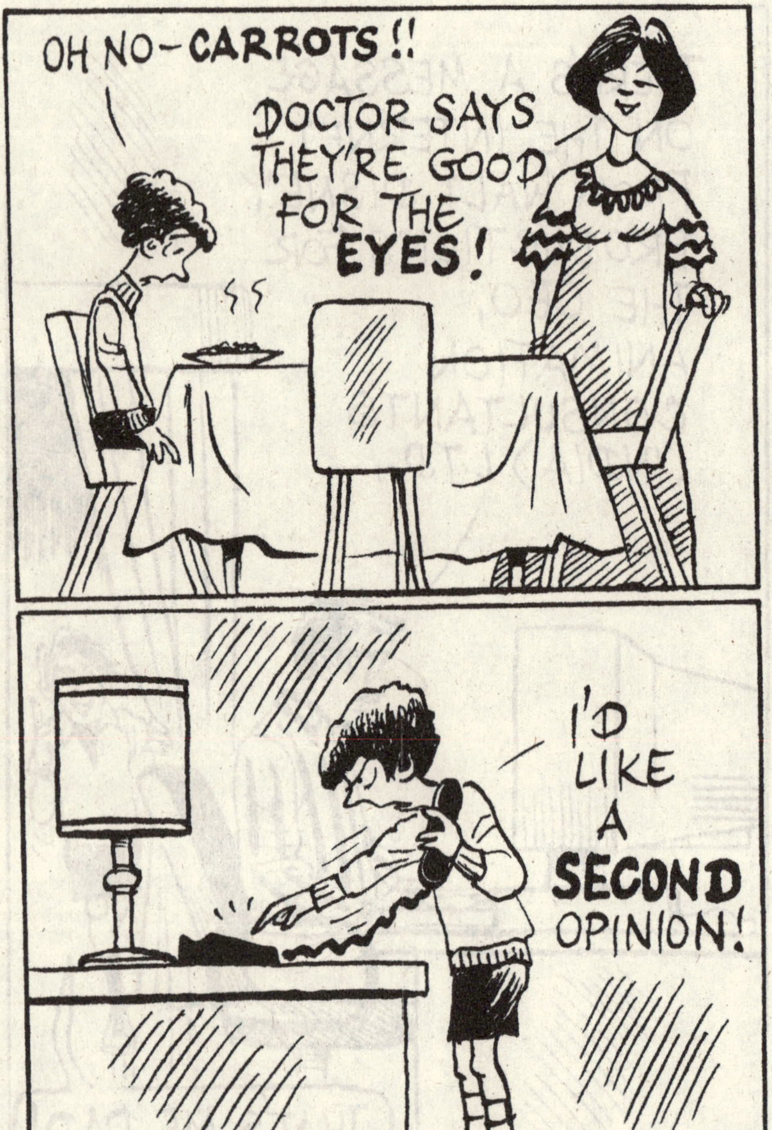
OH NO-CARROTS!!
DOCTOR SAYS THEY'RE GOOD FOR THE EYES!
I'D LIKE A SECOND OPINION!

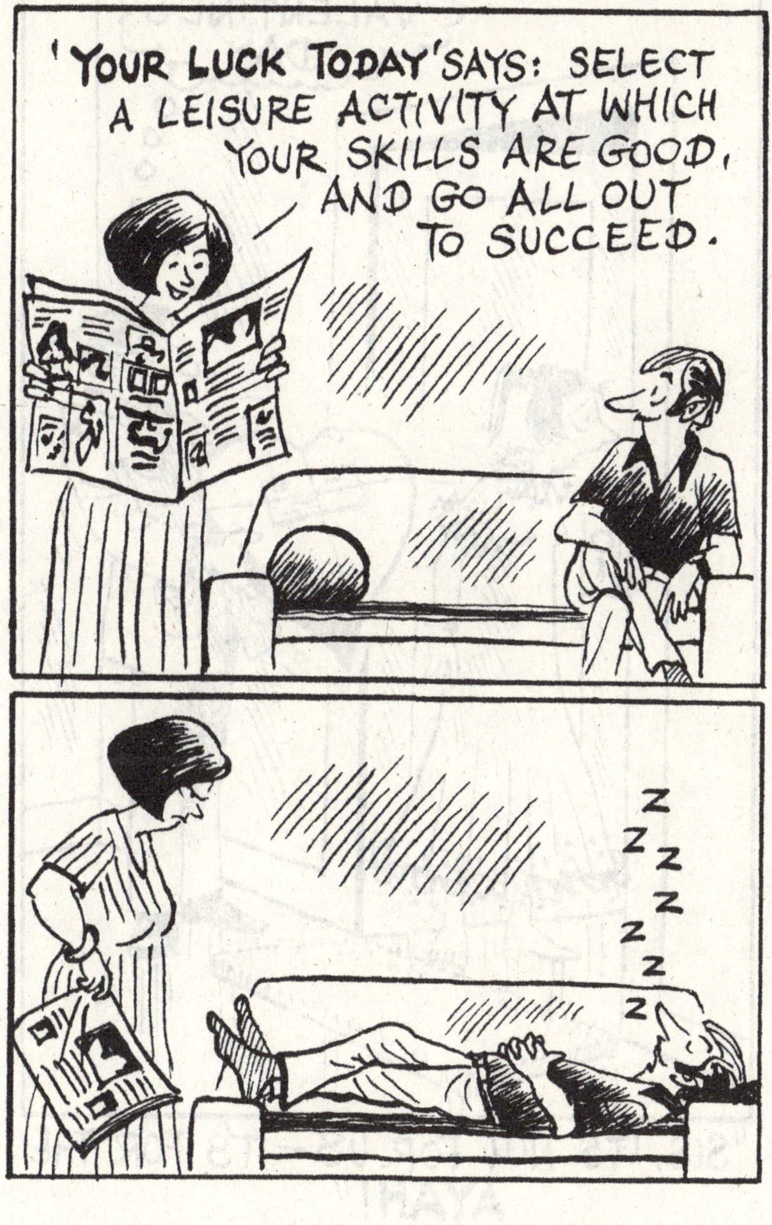
'YOUR LUCK TODAY' SAYS: SELECT A LEISURE ACTIVITY AT WHICH YOUR SKILLS ARE GOOD, AND GO ALL OUT TO SUCCEED.
Z Z Z Z Z Z Z

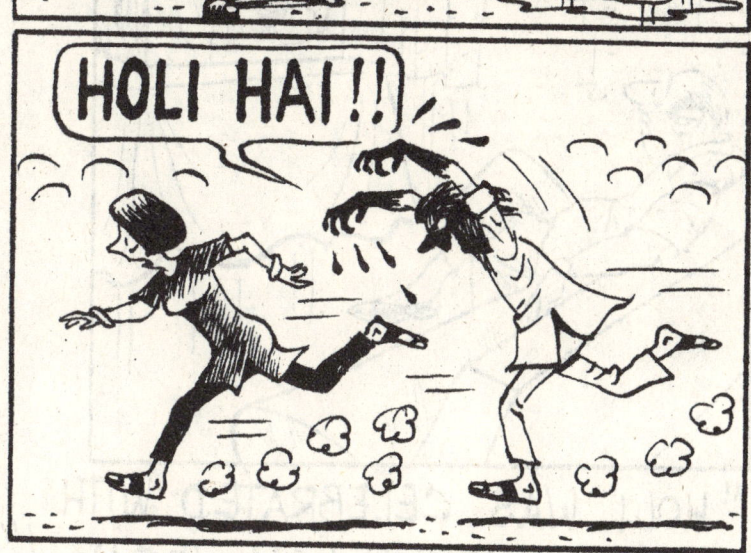

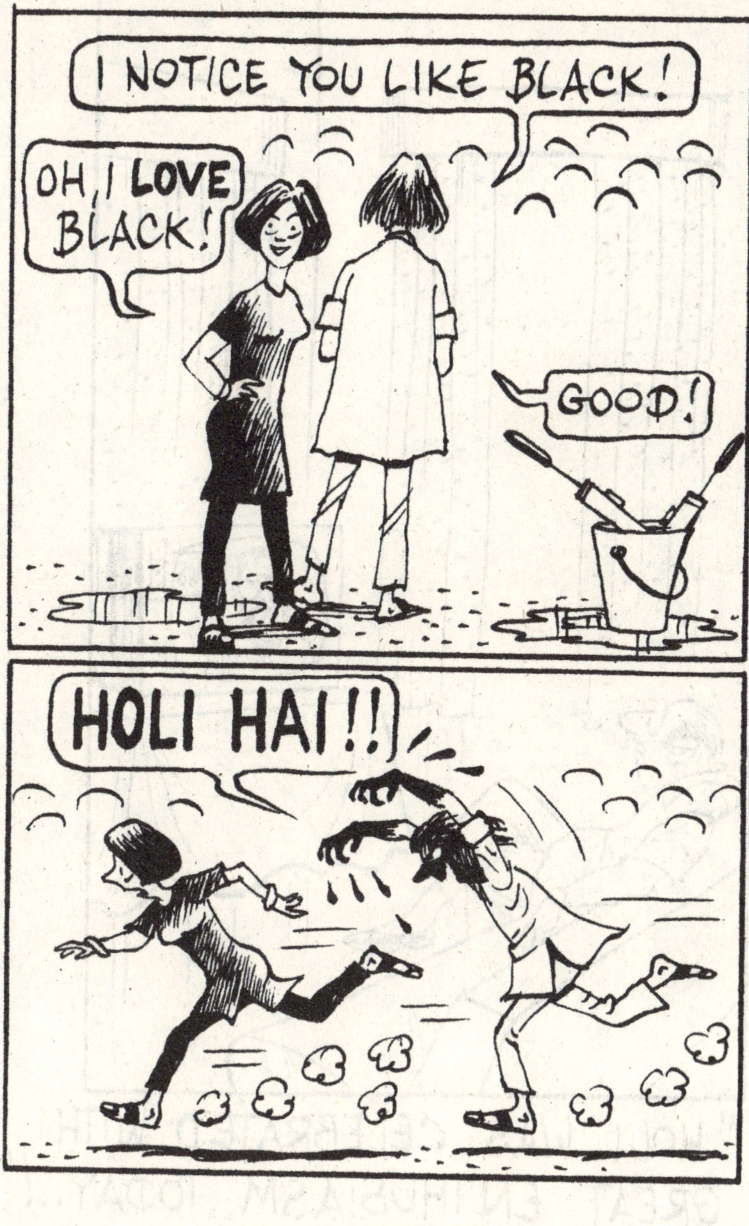

I NOTICE YOU LIKE BLACK!
OH, I **LOVE** BLACK!
GOOD!
HOLI HAI!!

"HOLI WAS CELEBRATED WITH GREAT ENTHUSIASM TODAY...!"

"MY DELEGATION AND I ARE HAPPY TO BE IN THE BEAUTIFUL CITY OF DELHI.."

"PLEASE, MADAM... COULD WE
HAVE YOUR AUTOGRAPH?!"

"KAUN BANEGA CROREPATI!!"

"GUESS WHO'S SPONSORING IT..!"

"...AND GETTING HAAT-ER!"

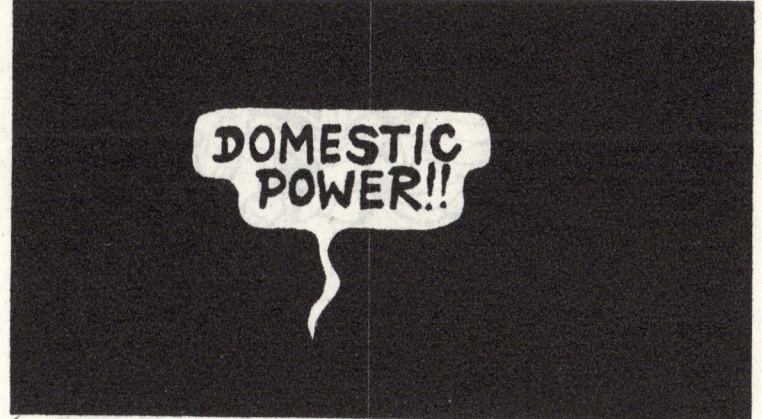

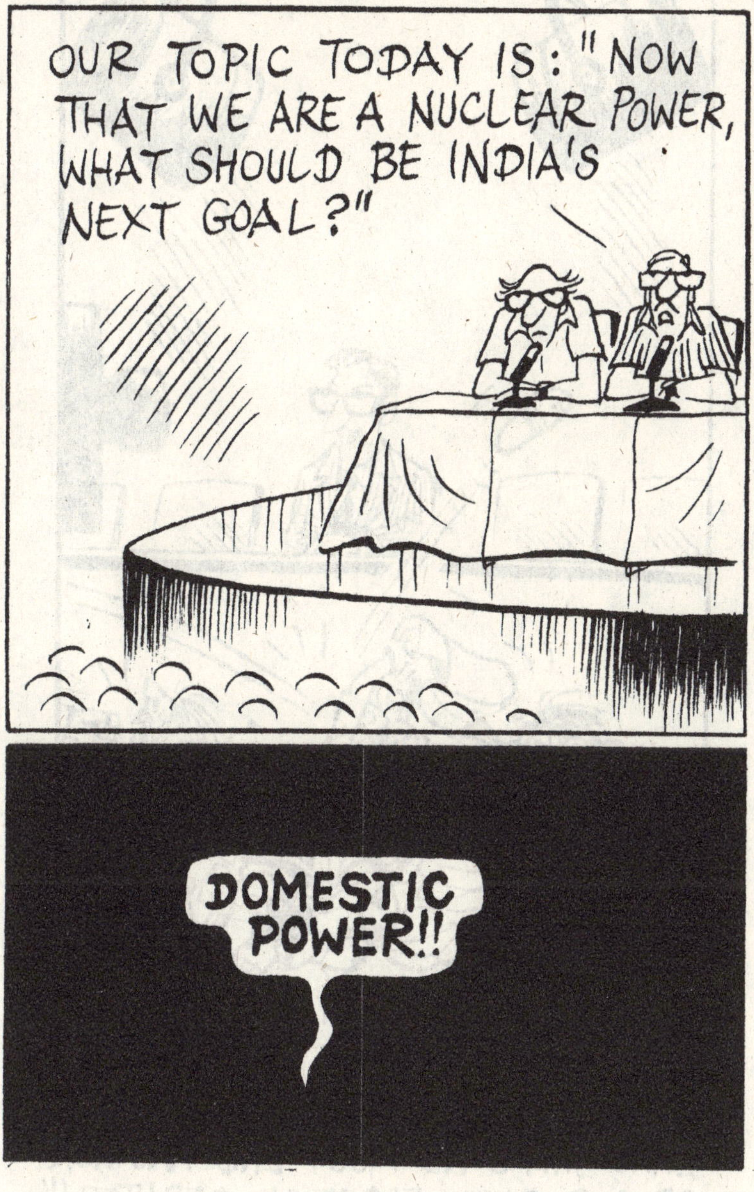
OUR TOPIC TODAY IS: "NOW THAT WE ARE A NUCLEAR POWER, WHAT SHOULD BE INDIA'S NEXT GOAL?"
DOMESTIC POWER!!

"..AND THERE WE MUST END ANOTHER OF OUR DAILY ELECTION DEBATES!"

"BECAUSE HE HATES SERIALS AND I HATE CRICKET!"

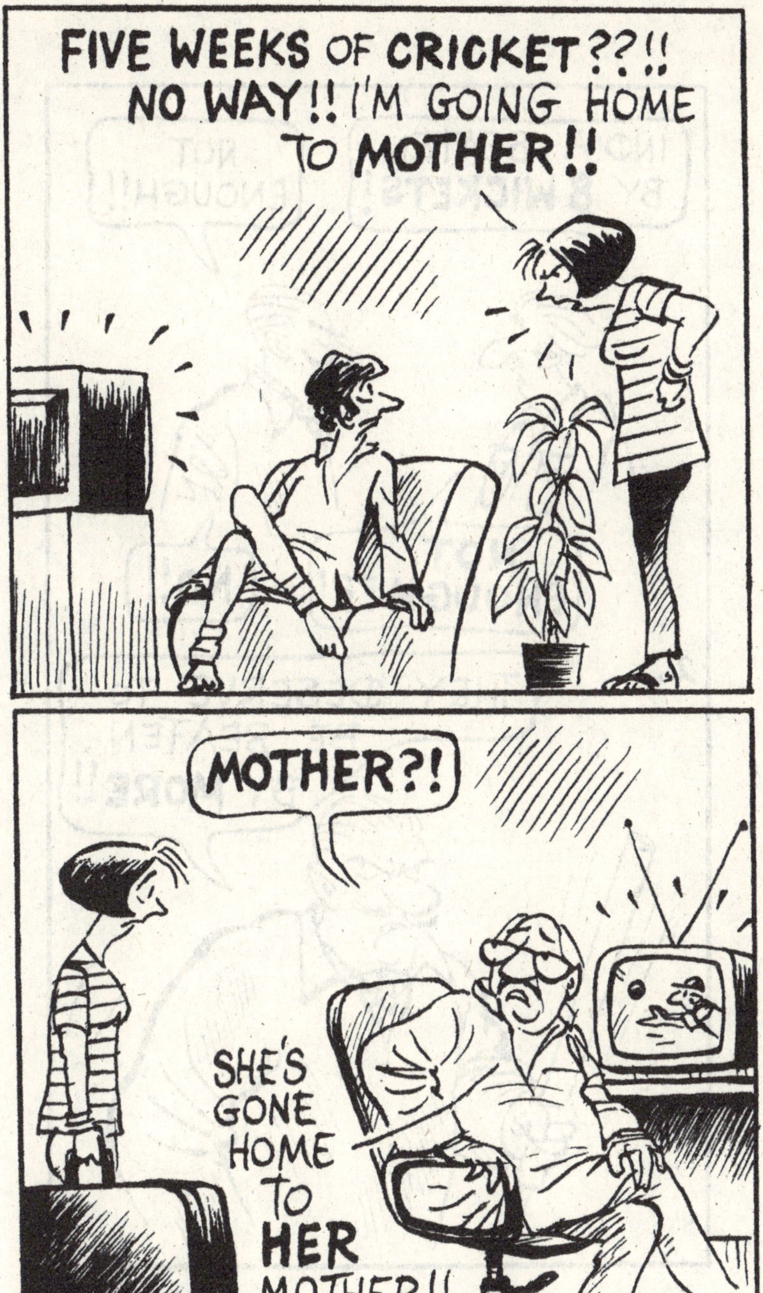
FIVE WEEKS OF CRICKET??!! NO WAY!! I'M GOING HOME TO MOTHER!!
MOTHER?!
SHE'S GONE HOME TO HER MOTHER!!

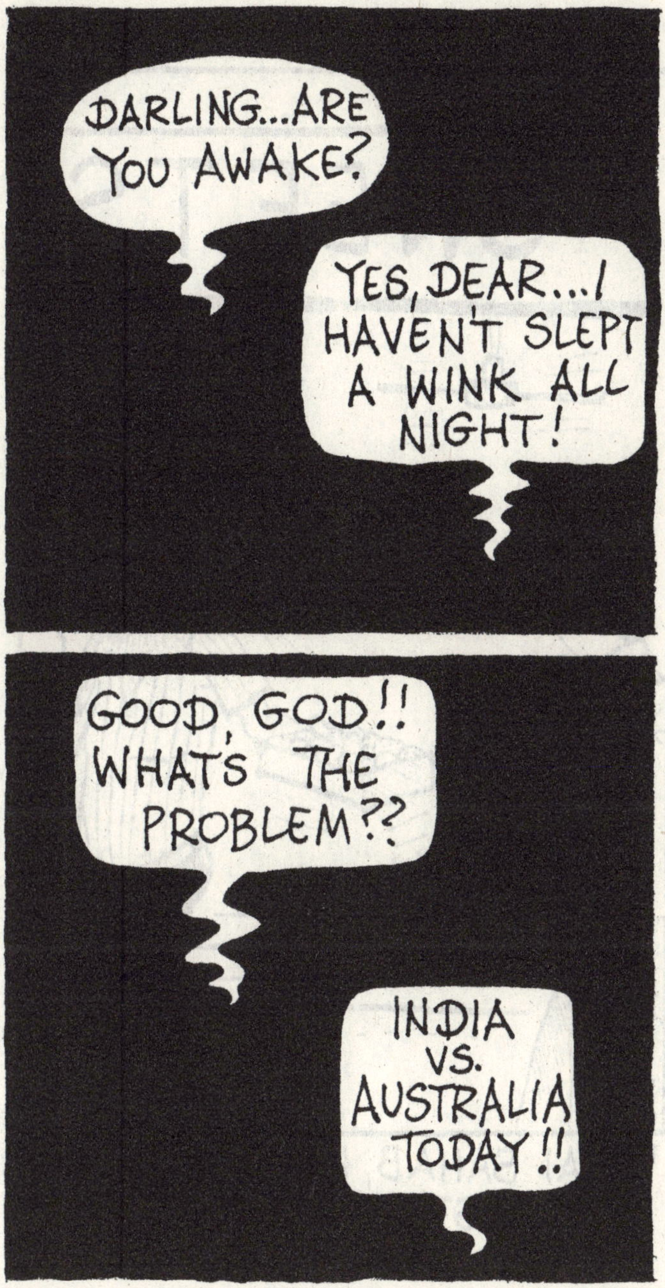
DARLING...ARE YOU AWAKE?
YES, DEAR...I HAVEN'T SLEPT A WINK ALL NIGHT!
GOOD GOD!! WHAT'S THE PROBLEM??
INDIA VS. AUSTRALIA TODAY!!

"BHAI SAHAB, HAVE A LADDOO..
AUSTRALIA'S OUT!"

"NEVER SEEN SUCH A BIASED UMPIRE..!"

"DON'T PLAY MISCHIEF! STOP QUOTING ME — YOU'RE GETTING ME INTO TROUBLE!"

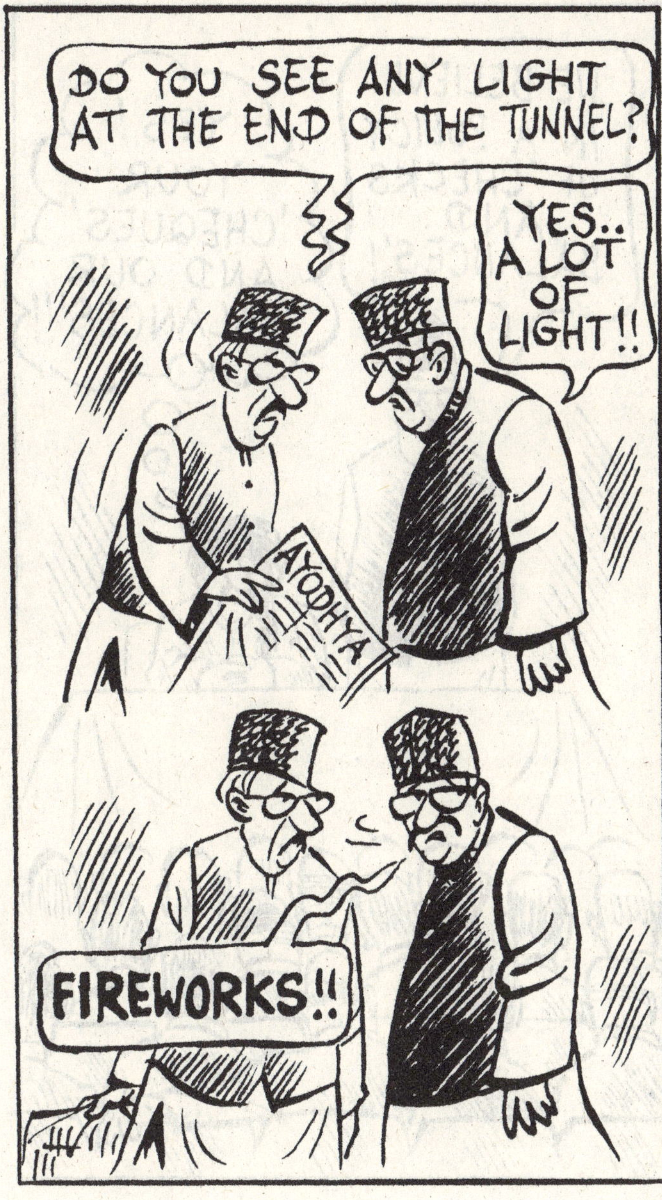
DO YOU SEE ANY LIGHT AT THE END OF THE TUNNEL?
YES.. A LOT OF LIGHT!!
AYODHYA
FIREWORKS!!

"ARRE, WHERE ARE YOU GOING WITH THAT CAP — YOU'RE IN **BJP** NOW!"

"THE JOB IS VERY CHALLENGING BUT I DIDN'T EXPECT SO MUCH SECURITY..!"

"COMPUTER, SIR!"

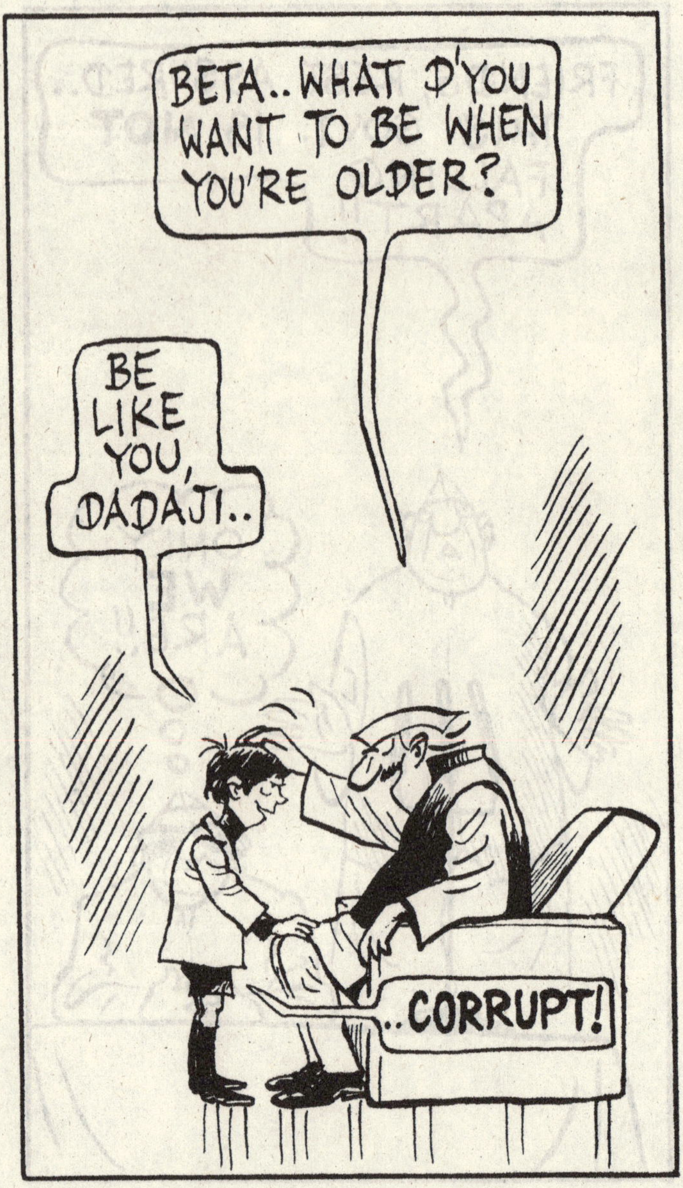
BETA..WHAT D'YOU WANT TO BE WHEN YOU'RE OLDER?
BE LIKE YOU, DADAJI..
..CORRUPT!

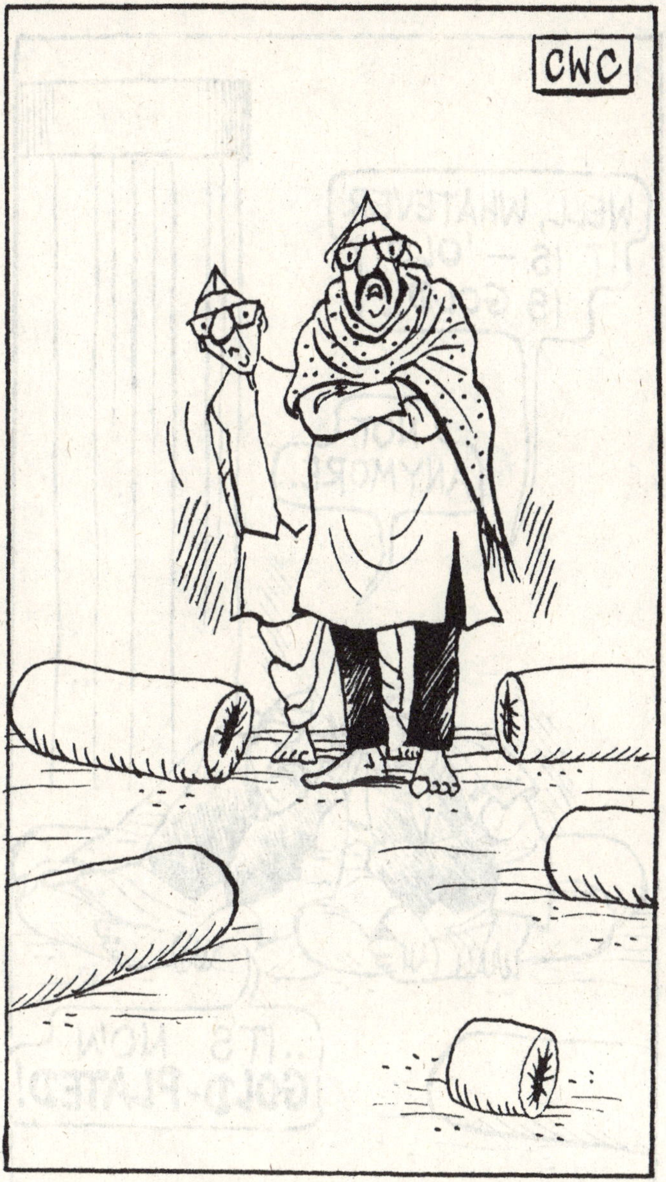
CWC

"HE'S BEEN CUT TO SIZE!"

"DAMMIT, OF COURSE THE MINISTER OF STATE KNOWS ME — WE WERE IN THE SAME **CELL** LAST YEAR!"

"IT'S FOR YOU — YOU'RE **SACKED!**"

"SOMEBODY SHOULD TELL MADAM- 'ROME WAS NOT BUILT IN A DAY'!"

"WE GIVE SUPPORT ONLY FROM 'OUTSIDE'... WE NEVER PROMISED ANY CO-OPERATION 'INSIDE'!"

"DON'T YOU DARE TOUCH THIS WILD, RAMPAGING MOB OF BLOODTHIRSTY GOONDAS—THEY'RE THE CM'S MEN!"

"LET'S GO TO ANOTHER PARK...
I **HATE** LOTUS!"

"NONSENSE!! THERE'S NO THREAT TO MY GOVT.!!"

"HOW CAN YOU EVER THINK OF A NO-CONFIDENCE MOTION AGAINST THE GOVT — WE'RE IN IT!"

"DEADWOOD! WHAT DEADWOOD?
SOLID TEAK!!"

"AH ... MR. 00647385491 !"

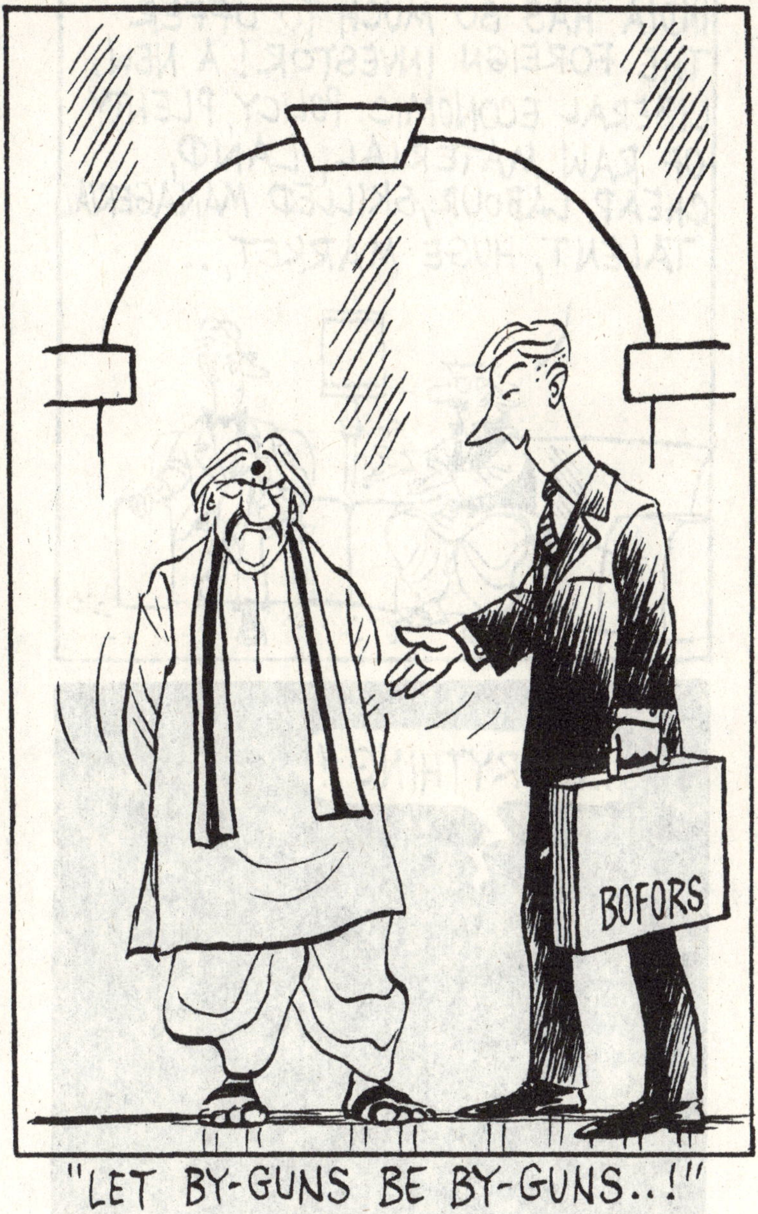
BOFORS
"LET BY-GUNS BE BY-GUNS..!"

"IN THIS CORRIDOR NOBODY CARES A DAMN ABOUT PAY— ONLY COMMISSION!"

"HE RETIRED AT 55..!"

"SORRY, MADAM, NO SMALL CHANGE... TAKE 'A BHINDI!"

"DON'T ASK.. IT'S NOT FOR THE POOR!"

"FINE...THAT TAKES CARE OF THE GOVERNMENT LIST!"

"BHAISAAB, THE PAKISTANIS WOULD PAY A FORTUNE FOR THIS— 'POKHARAN III'!"

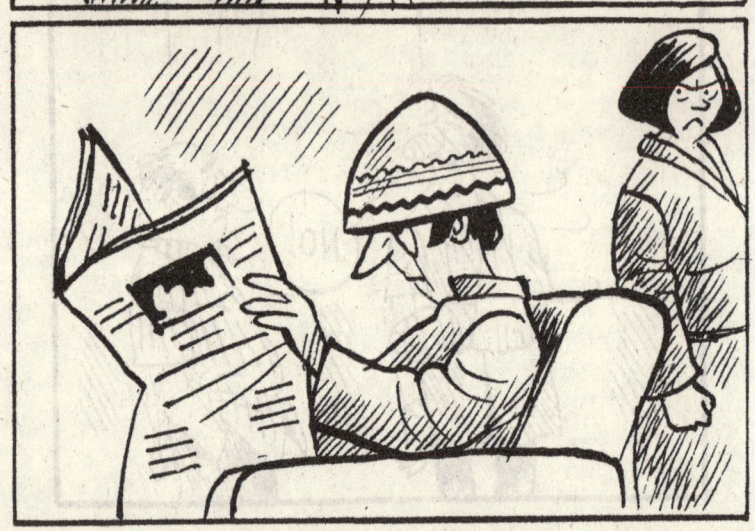

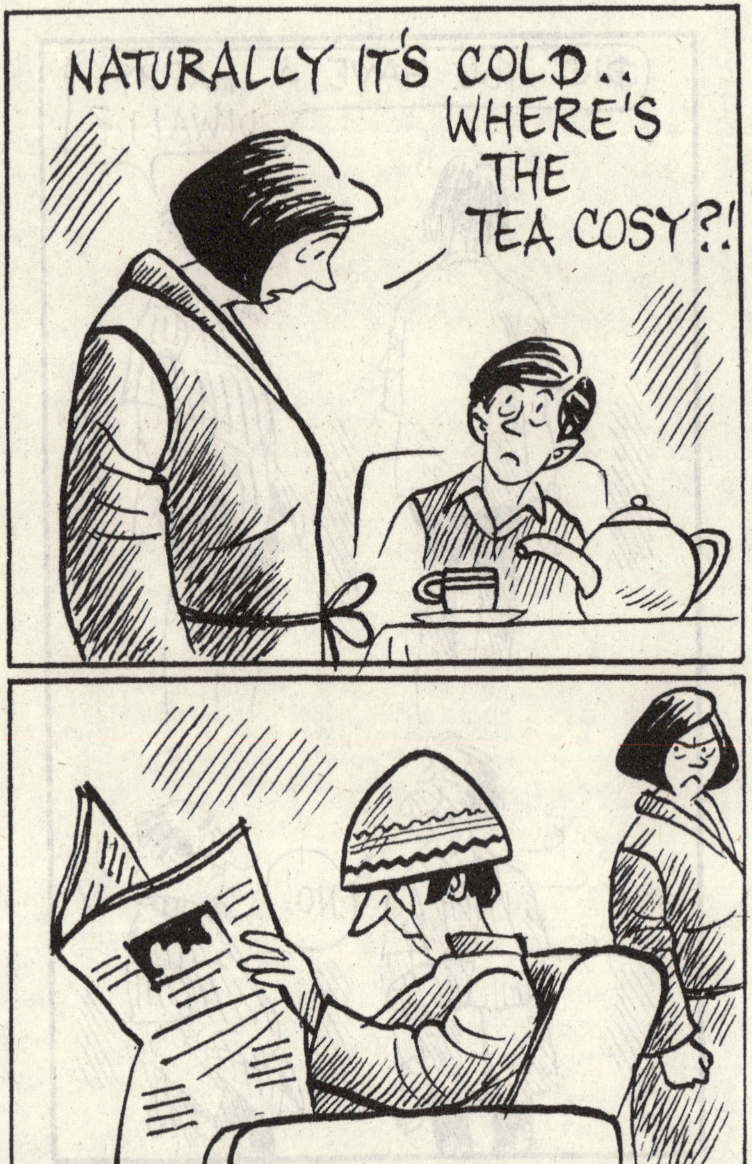
NATURALLY IT'S COLD..
WHERE'S THE TEA COSY?!

"TEA OR COFFEE?!"

"HAPPY NEW YEAR!"

"TONIGHT?? OH, JUST THE USUAL FAMILY GET-TOGETHER..!"